Sara Mason

Essence Pure
Natural Cosmetics
The Revolution in Personal Care

Original Title: Essence Pure: Natural Cosmetics
Copyright © 2025, published by Luiz Antonio dos Santos ME.

This book is a non-fiction work that explores practices and concepts in the field of natural cosmetics and holistic well-being. Through a comprehensive approach, the author offers practical tools to achieve emotional balance, self-care, and harmony with nature.

**1st Edition**
Production Team

**Author**: Sara Mason
**Editor**: Luiz Santos
**Cover**: Studios Booklas / Layout: Anna Fontana

**Publication and Identification**
Essence Pure: Natural Cosmetics - The Revolution in Personal Care
Booklas, 2025
Categories: Natural Cosmetics / Well-being / Holism
DDC: 646.7   - CDU: 391.5

**All rights reserved to:**
Luiz Antonio dos Santos ME / Booklas
No part of this book may be reproduced, stored in a retrieval system, or transmitted by any means — electronic, mechanical, photocopying, recording, or otherwise — without the prior express permission of the copyright holder.

# Summary

Systematic Index ........................................................................... 5
Prologue ......................................................................................... 9
Chapter 1 Holistic Beauty ........................................................... 11
Chapter 2 Natural Ingredients .................................................... 17
Chapter 3 Preparation and Conservation ................................. 23
Chapter 4 Skin: Types and Needs .............................................. 29
Chapter 5 Hair: Types and Care ................................................. 35
Chapter 6 Sensitivity Test ........................................................... 41
Chapter 7 Natural Facial Cleansing .......................................... 46
Chapter 8 Facial Exfoliation ....................................................... 51
Chapter 9 Facial Hydration ........................................................ 57
Chapter 10 Natural Facial Masks .............................................. 63
Chapter 11 Natural Facial Toner ............................................... 69
Chapter 12 Dark Circles and Bags ............................................ 76
Chapter 13 Acne Naturally ......................................................... 83
Chapter 14 Skin Spots ................................................................. 90
Chapter 15 Facial Rejuvenation ................................................. 96
Chapter 16 Natural Sun Protection ........................................... 102
Chapter 17 Body Scrub ............................................................... 108
Chapter 18 Body Hydration ....................................................... 114
Chapter 19 Cellulite: Natural Treatment .................................. 120
Chapter 20 Stretch Marks: Prevention and Treatment ............ 126
Chapter 21 Therapeutic Baths .................................................... 132
Chapter 22 Body Detoxification ................................................ 138
Chapter 23 Natural Hair Washing ............................................. 144

Chapter 24 Natural Conditioner ................................................. 149

Chapter 25 Natural Hair Masks ................................................ 154

Chapter 26 Natural Hair Finishing............................................. 159

Chapter 27 Hair Loss ................................................................ 165

Chapter 28 Dandruff and Scalp................................................. 171

Chapter 29 White Hair .............................................................. 177

Epilogue .................................................................................... 183

# Systematic Index

**Chapter 1: Holistic Beauty:** Explores beauty as an expression of integral well-being, transcending physical appearance and connecting body, mind and spirit.

**Chapter 2: Natural Ingredients:** Dives into the richness of natural ingredients, such as vegetable oils, butters, clays and extracts, which nourish, regenerate and protect skin and hair.

**Chapter 3: Preparation and Conservation:** Practical guide for the artisanal preparation of natural cosmetics, with tips on hygiene, utensils, techniques and conservation to ensure the quality of products.

**Chapter 4: Skin: Types and Needs:** Unravels the characteristics of different skin types and their specific needs, helping in the choice of products and personalized routines.

**Chapter 5: Hair: Types and Care:** Explores the structure and challenges of each hair type, with tips on natural care to maintain the health, strength and shine of the strands.

**Chapter 6: Sensitivity Test:** Addresses the importance of the sensitivity test to avoid allergic reactions and ensure the safe use of cosmetics, even natural ones.

**Chapter 7: Natural Facial Cleansing:** Presents natural methods and recipes for facial cleansing, with options for each skin type, promoting the removal of impurities and the balance of the skin.

**Chapter 8: Facial Exfoliation:** Details the benefits of facial exfoliation, which removes dead cells and stimulates cell renewal, with homemade recipes for each skin type.

**Chapter 9: Facial Hydration:** Highlights the importance of hydration for healthy and protected skin, with tips on products and natural recipes for every need.

**Chapter 10: Natural Facial Masks:** A guide on natural facial masks, which offer intensive treatment with nourishing ingredients and purifying clays, for radiant skin.

**Chapter 11: Natural Facial Toner:** Explains the role of facial toner in the care routine, balancing the skin's pH, controlling oiliness and preparing for hydration.

**Chapter 12: Dark Circles and Bags:** Addresses the causes of dark circles and bags, with care tips, natural recipes and healthy habits for a revitalized appearance.

**Chapter 13: Acne Naturally:** Explores the causes of acne and how to treat it naturally, with homemade recipes, skin care and diet tips for healthier skin.

**Chapter 14: Skin Spots:** Guide on the different types of skin blemishes, their causes and how to treat them with natural methods, promoting uniformity and lightening.

**Chapter 15: Facial Rejuvenation:** Addresses the skin aging process and how to care for mature skin with natural cosmetics, preventing wrinkles and revitalizing the appearance.

**Chapter 16: Natural Sun Protection:** Highlights the importance of sun protection and presents natural alternatives to protect the skin from the damage caused by UV rays.

**Chapter 17: Body Scrub:** Practical guide to body exfoliation, which removes dead cells, stimulates renewal and promotes softer, more even skin.

**Chapter 18: Body Hydration:** Emphasizes the importance of hydration for skin health, with tips on products and natural recipes to keep skin nourished and protected.

**Chapter 19: Cellulite: Natural Treatment:** Addresses the causes of cellulite and how to treat it naturally, with homemade recipes, massage tips and healthy habits to reduce the problem.

**Chapter 20: Stretch Marks: Prevention and Treatment:** Details the causes of stretch marks and how to prevent and treat them with natural methods, softening the appearance and improving skin texture.

**Chapter 21: Therapeutic Baths:** Explores the power of therapeutic baths with herbs and essential oils, promoting relaxation, well-being and energy balance.

**Chapter 22: Body Detoxification:** Guide on how to promote body detoxification naturally, with tips on nutrition, teas, juices and practices to eliminate toxins and revitalize the body.

**Chapter 23: Natural Hair Washing:** Presents natural methods for washing hair, with alternatives such as solid shampoos, No Poo and Co-Wash, for healthy and clean hair, without harming the environment.

**Chapter 24: Natural Conditioner:** Details the benefits of using natural conditioners, with nourishing and moisturizing ingredients, for soft, shiny and manageable hair.

**Chapter 25: Natural Hair Masks:** A guide on natural hair masks with nourishing and moisturizing ingredients for different hair types, promoting the health and beauty of the strands.

**Chapter 26: Natural Hair Finishing:** Addresses hair finishing with natural products, such as vegetable oils and gels, to shape, protect and shine hair, without the use of chemicals.

**Chapter 27: Hair Loss:** Analyzes the causes of hair loss and how to treat it with natural methods, strengthening the strands and promoting healthy growth.

**Chapter 28: Dandruff and Scalp:** Addresses scalp problems, such as dandruff and itching, with natural solutions to keep the scalp healthy and balanced.

**Chapter 29: White Hair:** Highlights specific care for white hair, with tips on hydration, nutrition and natural products to keep the color vibrant and the strands healthy.

Fontes e conteúdo relacionado

# Prologue

Imagine a universe where every touch on your skin, every aroma you inhale, and every choice you make in caring for yourself not only transforms your appearance but also connects you to something greater: the essence of a full life, balanced and in harmony with the world around you. This book is more than just a read; it is a portal to that universe.

Here, ancestral secrets and modern science unite to reveal transformative knowledge that goes far beyond what is visible in the mirror. Prepare to immerse yourself in a holistic approach that transcends mere aesthetic care. You will be invited to explore beauty as an expression of integral well-being, aligning body, mind, and spirit in a natural and harmonious flow.

Each page brings not only information but revelations. You will discover how simple and natural ingredients, long forgotten in a world dominated by artificiality, have the power to revitalize and renew not only the skin but also the connection with your own essence. The natural cosmetics presented here are not a passing fad; it is a return to wisdom, a rescue of respect for nature and for the body as a sacred temple.

By opening this book, you will allow yourself to go beyond the barriers imposed by rigid and unattainable standards. You will be led on a path of practical discoveries and deep reflections, ranging from the conscious choice of foods that nourish the skin from the inside to self-care rituals that promote inner peace. It is more than a beauty manual: it is an invitation to rethink your lifestyle, your priorities, and the way you relate to yourself and the planet.

The words here were not written just to be read, but to be lived. By applying the principles and techniques shared, you will feel a genuine transformation. Not only in the softness of your skin or the shine of your hair, but in the way you see and appreciate the world around you.

Allow yourself this journey. Be inspired by the alchemy of natural ingredients and the power of conscious choices. Accept this book as a guide that not only illuminates the path to authentic beauty, but also awakens a deep sense of respect and admiration for the wonder that is the human body and its intrinsic connection to nature.

Open this book with an open heart and mind, and prepare for an experience that will go far beyond what you imagined.

With deep admiration for your search,
Luiz Santos
Editor

# Chapter 1
# Holistic Beauty

Beauty represents a profound and multidimensional expression that reflects not only appearance, but also inner balance and vitality. Far from being a restricted or superficial concept, it is a manifestation of harmony between body, mind, and spirit, an integration that transcends the standards imposed by society and embraces the uniqueness of each individual. Instead of following stereotypical models, true beauty finds its roots in integral health, in connection with nature, and in the authenticity of living fully. It is a reflection of well-being that radiates from the inside out, built by conscious choices and habits that nurture all dimensions of being.

This broader understanding of beauty not only challenges old paradigms but also invites a profound transformation in the way we care for ourselves. Nourishing the body with proper nutrition, cultivating positive thoughts, and practicing self-care are practices that form the basis of a balanced and rewarding life. Beauty, in this context, ceases to be just an external pursuit and becomes a natural reflection of a peaceful and aligned interior. The glow of the skin, the strength of the hair, and the energy of the body become signs of this harmony, not isolated objectives.

Natural cosmetics emerge as a valuable ally on this path, offering a link between the human being and the resources of nature. Using ingredients that respect the environment and the needs of the body, it promotes care that goes beyond aesthetics and extends to global well-being. This approach not only rescues ancient traditions but also stimulates ecological awareness and the appreciation of sustainable processes. By choosing natural cosmetics, the individual reinforces a commitment to their own health and that of the planet, creating a virtuous cycle of care, respect, and true beauty.

Holistic beauty presents itself as a profound expression that goes beyond the limits of physical appearance, rooting itself in the essential connection between body, mind, and spirit. This integrative vision understands true beauty as a result of a state of inner harmony, where emotional, physical, and energetic balance align. It is a beauty that is not only reflected in the health of the skin, the shine of the hair, or the vitality of the body, but also in the serenity of a look, the lightness of movements, and the genuine joy of living. This concept transcends external demands, allowing beauty to manifest as a reflection of inner peace and alignment.

Within this approach, natural cosmetics stand out as a powerful ally in the search for this harmony. More than just products and techniques for external care, it offers a path to self-knowledge and to connection with nature and oneself. Based on natural ingredients, it respects the body, values the environment, and transforms the act of caring for oneself into a meaningful ritual. This care invites us to see our body as a sacred temple that deserves to be nurtured with love and respect, promoting a continuous cycle of well-being and beauty.

Holistic beauty is supported by fundamental pillars that guide both daily care and personal choices. Conscious nutrition is one of the main foundations, being the basis for health and balanced appearance. A diet rich in fruits, vegetables, whole grains, and quality proteins provides the body with the nutrients it needs to function fully. This care with food is reflected in luminous skin, strong hair, and healthy nails. Choosing organic and locally produced foods not only reinforces health, but also promotes a sustainable relationship with the environment, showing that food choices impact both the individual and the planet.

Another essential pillar is emotional balance. Negative emotions such as stress, anxiety, and anger can deeply impact the body, manifesting through wrinkles, acne, hair loss, and other imbalances. On the other hand, cultivating positive feelings such as joy, gratitude, and love is a practice that harmonizes the interior and is reflected in a more vibrant and healthy appearance. Practices such as meditation, yoga, moments outdoors, and pleasurable activities are effective ways to achieve this emotional harmony and, consequently, inner beauty.

Conscious movement also plays an indispensable role in this context. The human body was designed to move, and the regular practice of physical activities not only strengthens muscles and improves circulation, but also promotes the release of endorphins, which generate a feeling of well-being. Whether through dance, walking, swimming, or yoga, finding an enjoyable activity is essential to keep the body active and the mind in balance.

Restorative sleep is another fundamental pillar. During the hours of rest, the body carries out processes of cell regeneration and release of hormones vital for health and appearance. Quality sleep contributes to a rejuvenated and revitalized appearance, reinforcing the importance of creating a quiet and dark environment that favors deep rest. This care translates into benefits for the skin, for general health, and for the emotional state.

Connection with nature emerges as a crucial component for integral well-being. Being outdoors, breathing fresh air, feeling the sun on your skin, and observing the beauty of the natural world provides a sense of balance and tranquility. This relationship with nature is also strengthened by natural cosmetics, which use ingredients from sustainable sources to care for the skin and hair, promoting a connection with the environment and with our own essence.

Finally, conscious self-care represents an act of self-love that goes beyond simple care with appearance. It manifests itself in small daily moments that nourish the soul and promote well-being. Whether it's a relaxing bath, a pleasant read, or a skincare ritual with natural cosmetics, these practices connect us with our own unique beauty. By making self-care a priority, we celebrate life and reinforce our ability to radiate beauty and confidence.

Natural cosmetics, in particular, offer a return to origins, rescuing ancestral wisdom and the richness of natural ingredients. Vegetable oils, butters, clays, plant extracts, and essential oils are used to nourish, protect, and beautify in a sustainable way. Choosing products free of harsh chemicals not only promotes health, but also contributes to a positive impact on the environment, valuing conscious consumption and artisanal production practices.

The journey through holistic beauty is unique and personal, a process of discovery that does not follow fixed patterns, but that adjusts to the needs and desires of each individual. By nourishing the body, calming the mind, and aligning the spirit, each person finds their own expression of beauty, which radiates authenticity and well-being. Natural cosmetics are a tool on this journey, allowing self-care to also be a moment of celebration and connection with one's own essence.

This search transcends the physical, expressing itself in gestures, smiles, and looks that illuminate not only those who experience it, but also everyone around them. Holistic beauty, in its fullness, is an invitation to embrace uniqueness and to cultivate a state of balance and peace that transforms not only appearance, but also the quality of life and relationships with the world.

Holistic beauty also invites us to look beyond ourselves, understanding that our inner state directly influences the environment and the people around us.

When we take care of our emotional, physical, and spiritual health, we radiate an energy that inspires and uplifts those who are close. This overflow effect demonstrates that self-care is not a selfish act, but a practice that, by strengthening the individual, creates more meaningful and harmonious connections with the collective and with nature.

This path, although full of challenges, is deeply rewarding. Each conscious choice, from the food we consume to the products we apply to our skin, reflects a commitment to a fuller and more balanced life. It is these small gestures, often everyday, that build a solid foundation for a beauty that is not limited to the mirror, but that resonates as a transformative force in all areas of life. With each step, the journey through holistic beauty becomes a testament to authenticity, resilience, and self-love.

By integrating body, mind, and spirit, we discover that true beauty is timeless and unlimited. It resides in the uniqueness of each being, in the acceptance of imperfections, and in the appreciation of what is essential. This balance, which springs from within and manifests itself in every action, is proof that holistic beauty is not just an ideal to be achieved, but a way of living that allows us to flourish in our totality.

# Chapter 2
# Natural Ingredients

Natural ingredients used in cosmetics represent a true wealth of benefits, being versatile and adaptable elements that meet the most diverse personal care needs. Coming from sustainable sources and rich in nutrients, they are able to nourish, regenerate and protect the skin and hair, promoting not only beauty, but also integral health. This approach based on the simplicity and effectiveness of nature not only replaces the synthetic chemicals often found in conventional cosmetics, but also offers a care experience that respects the natural balance of the body and the environment. By opting for these ingredients, there is a valorization of organic processes and the innate properties that each plant or mineral has, transforming daily care into a ritual of connection with the essence of the earth.

Among the most valuable options in natural cosmetics are vegetable oils, vegetable butters, clays and hydrolats. Each category has a unique set of therapeutic properties, ranging from deep hydration to cell regeneration and the control of specific conditions, such as acne or extreme dryness. Vegetable oils, for example, stand out for their composition rich in essential fatty acids and antioxidants, offering effective hydration without clogging pores. Vegetable butters, with their dense and creamy texture, are ideal for intensive treatments, while clays, with their remineralizing properties, provide deep cleansing and renewal. Hydrolats, in turn, offer softness and freshness, acting as natural tonics to balance the pH of the skin.

The choice of natural ingredients also reflects a commitment to long-term well-being and sustainability. Each oil, butter or extract carries with it a history of traditional care and responsible use of nature's resources, promoting a virtuous cycle of conscious consumption. By incorporating these substances into everyday life, it is possible to observe results that go beyond appearance, reaching a state of internal and external balance. In addition, these ingredients not only care for the body, but also promote a positive impact on the environment, being biodegradable and coming from agricultural practices that respect the ecosystem. This union between functionality, respect for nature and well-being is what makes natural cosmetics such a powerful and transformative choice.

Natural ingredients are true jewels of cosmetics, offering a wide range of benefits for skin and hair care, always respecting the balance of the body and the environment. Each element, extracted from nature, carries within itself a unique set of therapeutic properties ranging from deep hydration to the treatment of specific conditions, such as acne, dryness and sensitivity. Choosing these ingredients is more than an aesthetic decision; it is a commitment to integral health and sustainability.

Vegetable oils, for example, stand out for their versatility and effectiveness. Extracted from plants, seeds and fruits, they are rich in fatty acids, vitamins and antioxidants, making them indispensable allies to nourish and protect the skin and hair. Coconut oil, with its rich composition in lauric acid, offers antibacterial and antifungal properties, being ideal for moisturizing and softening dry and sensitive skin. Its use goes beyond the skin, working as a massage oil, makeup remover and hair moisturizer. Argan oil, in turn, is a treasure originating from Morocco, known for its regenerating and anti-aging properties, being indicated for mature skin and weakened hair, to which it gives shine and strength.

Rosehip oil is widely used to treat scars, blemishes and stretch marks, thanks to its concentration of vitamin C and essential fatty acids. It not only regenerates the skin, but also prevents premature aging. Jojoba oil, with its light texture and composition similar to human sebum, is perfect for all skin types, especially oily and acne-prone skin, providing hydration without clogging pores. Finally, sweet almond oil, rich in vitamin E, offers emollient and soothing properties, being indicated for sensitive and delicate skin, in addition to being an excellent oil for massages.

Vegetable butters, with their dense texture and nourishing properties, offer intensive care for dry skin and damaged hair. Shea butter, rich in vitamins A, E and F, deeply hydrates, regenerates and heals, being especially effective in treating cracks and roughness. Cocoa butter, with its antioxidant properties, prevents skin dryness, improves elasticity and protects against free radical damage. Mango butter, in turn, combines hydration and antioxidant action, being ideal to prevent premature aging and promote skin elasticity.

Another group of valuable ingredients are clays, natural minerals that cleanse, purify and remineralize the skin. Green clay, rich in silicon, aluminum and magnesium, is the ideal choice for oily and acne-prone skin, helping to control oiliness and treat acne. White clay, with its lightening and softening properties, is perfect for sensitive and blemished skin, promoting an even and hydrated appearance. Pink clay, a mixture of white and red clays, combines softness and healing action, being indicated for delicate skin and with rosacea, as it soothes and revitalizes.

Hydrolats, also known as floral waters, are a gentle and aromatic way to benefit the skin. Obtained during the distillation of aromatic plants, they have specific therapeutic properties. Lavender hydrolat, with its calming and healing action, is ideal for sensitive and acne-prone skin, reducing irritation and aiding in skin regeneration. Rose hydrolat, rich in moisturizing and regenerating properties, is a natural tonic for dry and mature skin, promoting luminosity and revitalization. Chamomile hydrolat is an ally for irritated and allergy-prone skin, soothing, softening and promoting healing.

Plant extracts, concentrated in active ingredients, offer specific solutions for different needs. Aloe vera extract deeply hydrates, soothes irritation and aids in healing, making it ideal for sensitive and acne-prone skin. Calendula extract is a powerful healer and anti-inflammatory, indicated for skin with wounds, dermatitis or irritation. Chamomile extract, with its antiallergic and calming action, is perfect for relieving redness and itching, providing immediate comfort.

Finally, essential oils are the protagonists of aromatherapy and natural cosmetics, offering powerful benefits in low concentrations. Lavender essential oil, with its calming and relaxing properties, is one of the most versatile, and can be used to soothe the skin, relieve tension and promote general well-being.

These natural ingredients, in addition to promoting visible results on the skin and hair, connect the user to the ancestral wisdom of nature and respect for the environment. Incorporating them into everyday life is an invitation to transform personal care into a ritual of conscious self-care, where functionality, sustainability and well-being meet.

Natural ingredients, with their rich diversity, prove to be powerful allies not only for external care, but also for connection with the essence and natural rhythms of the body. By using them, we enter a universe of possibilities where each element carries within itself the wisdom of the earth, allowing personal care to become a moment of introspection and harmony. More than treating the skin or hair, these ingredients invite us to adopt conscious practices that reflect a reverence for nature and a commitment to balance between man and the environment.

This care goes beyond visible results, encouraging a deeper relationship with one's own body and with the planet. Choosing natural ingredients is opting for a path that values sustainability and tradition, without giving up efficacy. Each oil, butter, clay or extract used carries a history of ancestral use that resists time, bringing proven benefits and respecting the uniqueness of each individual. Thus, the act of taking care of oneself also becomes a celebration of the natural and cultural heritage that connects us to the past and the future.

By integrating natural ingredients into the routine, we discover that self-care is more than a habit - it is a ritual that nourishes both the skin and the soul. The transformation that these elements provide transcends appearance, promoting a feeling of global well-being. In this process, we are reminded that true beauty is rooted in conscious choices, respect for nature and the authenticity of each gesture, creating a cycle of balance and fullness.

# Chapter 3
# Preparation and Conservation

Preparing natural cosmetics is an act that combines creativity, knowledge and self-care, providing a level of control and personalization that can hardly be achieved with commercial products. More than a craft practice, this experience allows connection with the pure ingredients of nature and the development of formulas adapted to your specific needs. The choice of each element - be it a nutrient-rich vegetable oil, a deeply moisturizing butter or an infusion of herbs with therapeutic properties - reflects a commitment to the health of the skin and body, as well as a respect for sustainability and simplicity.

The preparation process requires not only attention to the ingredients, but also care with the space and utensils used. A clean and organized environment is essential to avoid contamination and ensure the quality of the final product. In addition, precision is fundamental in natural cosmetics. Each exact measurement contributes to the balance of the formulation, while the use of appropriate utensils, such as precision scales, glass or stainless steel bowls and storage bottles, ensures that the product is safe and effective. This attention to detail transforms the practice into an almost meditative ritual, which values each step of the process.

Conservation is another crucial point for the success of natural cosmetics. Because they are free of synthetic preservatives, homemade products have a shorter shelf life, which requires careful techniques to prolong their durability. The use of dark glass packaging, storage in cool places and the addition of natural preservatives, such as vitamin E and vegetable extracts, are measures that help to preserve the quality of cosmetics. At the same time, keeping track of the expiration date and observing changes in the appearance or aroma of products are important habits to ensure their safety. This care, in addition to prolonging the shelf life of formulations, reinforces the idea that natural cosmetics is not just a beauty alternative, but also a path to more conscious practices aligned with nature.

Preparing natural cosmetics is an enriching experience that unites creativity, care and respect for nature. This process not only allows the creation of personalized products, but also promotes a unique connection with the pure elements of the earth. However, to achieve safe and effective results, it is essential to pay attention to the workspace, the utensils used, the preparation techniques and the conservation of the products, ensuring that each step is carried out with care and precision.

Before you start, organize the environment in which you will be working. Choose a clean, well-lit and airy place, preferably away from sources of contamination. Make sure all utensils, ingredients and packaging are available, minimizing interruptions during preparation. Cleaning the space and organizing materials are not just details; they are fundamental steps for the safety and quality of the cosmetics produced.

Some utensils are indispensable for practice. A precision scale is essential for measuring ingredients, especially essential oils, which require exact doses. Measuring cups and spoons are useful for measuring liquids and solids, while spatulas and glass or stainless steel bowls are ideal for mixing the components. Avoid the use of plastics, as they can react with natural ingredients. For heating ingredients, such as butters and waxes, prefer enamel or stainless steel pans in a bain-marie. Dark glass packaging, in turn, protects cosmetics from light, preserving their properties. Don't forget to label each product with the name, date of manufacture and expiration date.

Hygiene is one of the pillars in the production of natural cosmetics. Wash your hands carefully and disinfect utensils and surfaces with 70% alcohol. To eliminate microorganisms, sterilize items that will come into direct contact with the final products. This can be done by boiling the utensils in water for 15 minutes or using a steam sterilizer. The use of disposable gloves is recommended, especially when handling essential oils or ingredients that may cause irritation. Masks are also useful to avoid inhaling fine particles during preparation.

Accuracy in measuring ingredients is crucial. Familiarize yourself with the most common conversions, such as 1 tablespoon (15 ml), 1 teaspoon (5 ml) and 1 drop of essential oil (approximately 0.05 ml). Following the proportions indicated in the recipes ensures that the final product is balanced and safe.

Preparation techniques vary according to the formulation. One of the most common is simple mixing, where the ingredients are combined and homogenized. Bain-marie heating is used to melt butters and waxes, ensuring even incorporation. Infusion and maceration are effective methods for extracting the active ingredients from plants, whether using hot or cold liquids. These processes require patience and precision, but the result is a product rich in therapeutic properties.

The conservation of natural cosmetics is a challenge that requires special attention. Because they are free of synthetic preservatives, these products have a shorter shelf life. Use dark glass bottles to protect them from light and store them in cool, dry places, away from bathroom humidity, which can encourage the proliferation of microorganisms. Some cosmetics, such as creams and masks, can be kept in the refrigerator to prolong their shelf life. The inclusion of natural preservatives, such as vitamin E, tea tree essential oil or grapefruit seed extract, also helps to extend the shelf life of products.

It is essential to keep track of the manufacture and expiration dates of each cosmetic, noting this information on the labels. Observe the products regularly and discard those that show changes in color, odor or texture, as this may indicate deterioration.

Finally, adopting good manufacturing practices increases the quality and safety of your work. Use fresh, quality ingredients, strictly follow recipe measurements, and maintain hygiene of space and utensils. Preparing natural cosmetics is a continuous learning process, full of experimentation and discovery.

With these guidelines, you can create natural cosmetics that not only care for your skin and hair, but also reflect your commitment to well-being and sustainability. Turn this act into a moment of self-care and celebration, exploring the infinite possibilities that the ingredients of nature have to offer.

Preparing and preserving natural cosmetics is, above all, a practice that requires patience, dedication and an attentive eye to detail. Each stage of the process, from the choice of ingredients to the final storage, carries within it the opportunity to create products that go beyond the functional, transforming themselves into true extensions of personal care and connection with nature. Over time, learning expands, allowing for greater creativity and refinement in formulations, always in harmony with the principles of sustainability and respect for the environment.

In addition, this practice encourages a more intimate relationship with one's own body and its needs, as each recipe can be adjusted to meet individual needs. The search for fresh, quality ingredients not only ensures effective results, but also reinforces the importance of conscious choices in a world where sustainable consumption is increasingly essential. This commitment to quality and respect for the planet transforms the preparation of cosmetics into a meaningful and deeply satisfying ritual.

The beauty of preparing and preserving natural cosmetics lies in its simplicity and the greater purpose it represents. It is not just about manufacturing products for daily use, but about cultivating a self-care mindset that values nature and its impact on our lives. Each creation is a reflection of this philosophy, a celebration of balance, care and creativity that resonates far beyond immediate results, contributing to a fuller and more conscious lifestyle.

# Chapter 4
# Skin: Types and Needs

The skin is a visible reflection of internal balance and a vital system of protection and communication between the body and the environment. More than just a barrier, it plays fundamental roles ranging from thermoregulation to immune response, and its health is a direct indicator of overall well-being. Understanding the nuances of the skin, such as its layers and types, is essential to meet its specific demands and maintain its functionality. At the same time, caring for the skin involves more than just applying products; it is a commitment to conscious practices that value nutrition, protection, and regeneration, elements that natural cosmetics can offer with excellence.

Each layer of the skin performs an interconnected and crucial function. The epidermis protects the body against external agents and minimizes water loss, while the dermis, rich in collagen and elastin, provides support and elasticity, making it essential in the prevention of signs of aging. In turn, the hypodermis functions as an energy reserve and a thermal insulator. Understanding how these layers interact allows us to address the skin's needs holistically, promoting both health and beauty. Thus, daily care must be designed to preserve this complex structure, prioritizing the balance between hydration, nutrition, and defense against external aggressions.

The particularities of each skin type highlight the importance of a personalized approach, which recognizes individual differences and integrates them into an effective routine. Dry skin, for example, requires deep hydration and lipid replenishment, while oily skin requires sebum control and purification. For combination skin, the challenge is to balance areas with different needs, while sensitive skin needs extra attention and soothing ingredients. In this context, natural cosmetics stand out by offering ingredients that work in synergy with the skin's biology, such as vegetable oils, clays, and hydrolates, which meet these demands in a gentle and effective way. In this way, skin care becomes a journey of self-knowledge and connection with nature, reflecting health and vitality in every detail.

The skin is a complex organ whose health reflects the overall balance of the body. More than a protective barrier, it performs crucial functions such as thermal regulation, sensory perception, and immune response. Understanding its structure and specific needs is the first step in developing care that promotes not only beauty but also integral health. Natural cosmetics, with their holistic approach, offer effective solutions that work in synergy with the skin's biology, respecting its balance and supporting its natural functions.

The skin is composed of three main layers, each with interconnected roles. The epidermis, the outermost layer, acts as a shield against external agents, minimizing water loss and protecting against environmental damage. Its structure includes keratinocytes, which produce keratin, and melanocytes, which generate melanin, providing color and protection against sunlight. Below, the dermis provides support and elasticity to the skin, thanks to the presence of collagen and elastin fibers. This layer also houses blood vessels, glands, and nerve endings, playing an essential role in hydration and tissue repair. Finally, the hypodermis, formed mainly by adipose tissue, functions as a thermal insulator and energy reserve, in addition to protecting deeper structures.

Understanding skin types is essential to provide adequate and effective care. Classified according to sebum production, the main types are normal, dry, oily, combination, and sensitive. Normal skin is balanced, with a smooth texture, elasticity, and natural glow. Dry skin, on the other hand, has low sebum production, which results in flaking, a feeling of tightness, and greater sensitivity. Oily skin, in contrast, produces excess sebum, characterized by intense shine, dilated pores, and a tendency to acne. Combination skin combines characteristics of dry and oily skin, with the T-zone (forehead, nose, and chin) being oilier and the cheeks drier. Finally, sensitive skin is reactive to external stimuli, presenting redness, itching, and irritation.

To identify your skin type, a practical method is the tissue paper test. After washing your face with a neutral soap, dry it gently and wait about an hour. Press a tissue on the different areas of your face. If the tissue shows no oil, the skin is dry. If there is oiliness in the T-zone, it is combination skin. Generalized oiliness indicates oily skin.

Each skin type has specific needs that should guide the choice of products and the development of care routines. Normal skin requires maintenance of hydration and protection, with gentle and non-comedogenic products. Dry skin needs intense hydration and lipid replenishment, using formulas rich in emollients and humectants, while oily skin requires sebum control, purification, and acne prevention, with oil-free and astringent products. For combination skin, the challenge is to balance the different needs of the different areas of the face, while sensitive skin requires special attention, with hypoallergenic and soothing products.

Natural cosmetics offer a wide range of ingredients adapted to each skin type. Vegetable oils, butters, clays, hydrolates, and extracts are combined to meet these needs effectively and gently. For normal skin, ingredients such as jojoba oil, coconut oil, and lavender hydrolate are ideal. Dry skin benefits from shea butter, argan oil, and rose hydrolate, while oily skin finds balance with green clay, tea tree essential oil, and green tea extract. Combination skin can be treated with white clay, geranium hydrolate, and chamomile extract, and sensitive skin is soothed with pink clay, calendula oil, and chamomile hydrolate.

A basic care routine is essential for any skin type. Start with cleansing, removing impurities, makeup, and excess oil. Exfoliation, performed once or twice a week, helps to eliminate dead cells and stimulate cell renewal. Toning is an important step to balance the skin's pH and prepare it for the next products. Then, hydration replenishes water and nutrients, keeping the skin soft and protected. Finally, sunscreen is essential to prevent premature aging, blemishes, and the risk of skin cancer.

With these practices and an understanding of the particularities of the skin, it is possible to create a personalized care routine that promotes health, balance, and beauty. By opting for natural ingredients, you not only take care of your skin, but also connect to a sustainable and conscious approach, transforming daily care into a moment of self-knowledge and well-being.

The skin, in its complexity, reveals not only the internal state of the body, but also the influence of external factors, such as pollution, solar radiation, and stress. Therefore, caring for it requires a dynamic and integrated approach, which considers changes over time and responses to different stimuli. Knowledge about skin types and their specific needs allows us to create strategies that not only solve immediate problems, but also prevent future imbalances, promoting lasting and healthy beauty.

The conscious choice of appropriate products and routines is fundamental to respect the uniqueness of each skin. Opting for natural ingredients not only reduces the risk of irritation and allergies, but also strengthens the skin by working in harmony with its biological functions. This integrated care, which combines science and nature, reflects a gentler and more effective way to promote skin health, ensuring visible results and a sense of well-being that goes beyond the surface.

Caring for the skin is a gesture of self-care that invites us to slow down and observe our real needs. In this process, natural cosmetics act as a powerful ally, rescuing ancestral wisdom and combining it with contemporary advances. By incorporating conscious practices and pure ingredients, we transform the daily routine into a ritual of celebrating the connection between body, mind, and nature, reflecting the essence of a balance that transcends the physical.

# Chapter 5
# Hair: Types and Care

Hair, in addition to composing visual identity and expressing personality, performs important protective functions for the scalp. Its structure and appearance reflect both the overall health of the body and the care directed at it. The beauty and vitality of the strands do not depend only on genetic factors, but also on conscious practices appropriate to their individual characteristics. Understanding the structure of hair and its different curvatures is fundamental to adopting a routine that respects its needs and promotes natural balance, strength, and shine. In this context, natural cosmetics emerge as an effective and sustainable approach, allowing us to care for the hair with ingredients that nourish and protect in a genuine way.

The hair structure, formed by interdependent layers, requires attention to maintain its integrity. The cuticle, the outer layer composed of overlapping scales, protects the cortex and is responsible for the shine and resistance of the strands. When healthy, the cuticle reflects light, giving the hair a luminous and vibrant appearance. The cortex, located below the cuticle, gives strength and elasticity to the strands, in addition to determining their color through melanin. Finally, the medulla, when present, contributes to the density and thermal insulation of the hair. Caring for these layers with natural ingredients ensures the maintenance of these functions and protects the strands from damage caused by external agents.

Each hair type - straight, wavy, curly, or coily - has its own characteristics and challenges, which can be aggravated by factors such as sun exposure, use of inappropriate products, hormonal changes, and eating habits. While straight hair may be more prone to oiliness, curly and coily hair often face dryness due to the difficulty of natural sebum reaching the entire length of the strands. Choosing vegetable oils, butters, and extracts appropriate for each hair type is essential to meet these demands. Ingredients such as coconut oil for deep nourishment, shea butter for intense hydration, and aloe vera extract for revitalization are examples of natural allies that provide remarkable results without the harmful effects of chemical substances.

Adopting a personalized routine that combines gentle cleansing, regular hydration, nutrition, and protection is essential to preserve hair health. Natural products, such as sulfate-free shampoos, moisturizing masks made with fruits and essential oils for finishing, transform hair care into an enriching and sustainable experience. In addition, simple practices such as avoiding excessive use of heat tools, rinsing the strands with lukewarm water, and respecting the ideal washing frequency contribute to the longevity and beauty of the hair. Thus, by combining the wisdom of nature with conscious habits, it is possible to achieve healthy, vibrant, and full of life hair.

Hair is more than just an element of personal expression; it performs important protective functions and reflects the overall health and well-being of the body. Its complex structure and the differences between hair types require specific care that considers both its natural characteristics and the external factors that affect it. Natural cosmetics, with their pure ingredients and sustainable techniques, offer effective solutions to care for hair while promoting balance and health.

The structure of hair is composed of two main parts. The hair follicle, located in the dermis, is where the strands are formed and grow. It houses cells that produce keratin, the structural protein that gives hair strength and resilience. The hair shaft, the visible part of the strand, is composed of three layers. The cuticle, the outer layer formed by overlapping scales, protects the cortex and determines the shine and resistance of the strands. The cortex, the middle layer, is responsible for elasticity, strength, and color, being rich in melanin, the natural pigment of hair. The medulla, present in some types of strands, is less understood, but is believed to contribute to density and thermal insulation.

Hair types are classified according to their curvature, which directly influences their needs and challenges. Straight hair (type 1) has straight strands and tends to be oily at the root but dry at the ends, due to the ease with which natural sebum travels its length. Wavy hair (type 2) forms "S" waves and can have frizz and dryness at the ends. Curly hair (type 3) has spiral curls, which tend to be drier due to the difficulty of natural sebum reaching the ends, and usually have frizz. Coily hair (type 4) has tightly coiled curls or a coily texture, being extremely dry and more fragile, with a great need for hydration, nutrition, and reconstruction.

For each hair type, there is specific care that meets its particular needs. Straight hair requires control of oiliness at the root and hydration of the ends, with light products that do not weigh down the strands. Wavy hair needs frizz control and hydration to define the waves. Curly hair requires deep hydration, nutrition, and products that define the curls, reducing frizz. Coily hair, in turn, requires intensive hydration, frequent nutrition, and protection against dryness, in addition to regular reconstructions to strengthen the strands.

In addition to the natural characteristics of the strands, other factors influence their health, such as genetics, diet, hormonal changes, and stress levels. Inadequate habits, such as washing hair with very hot water, using harsh products, or tying wet hair, can also cause significant damage. It is essential to align healthy practices with the choice of natural and appropriate products to preserve hair integrity.

Natural cosmetics offer an arsenal of powerful ingredients to care for hair effectively and sustainably. Vegetable oils, such as coconut, argan, castor, jojoba, and avocado, are rich in nutrients and help nourish and strengthen the strands. Vegetable butters, such as shea, cocoa, and cupuaçu, provide intense hydration and protection against dryness. Plant extracts, such as aloe vera, chamomile, and rosemary, revitalize and stimulate healthy growth. Other natural ingredients, such as honey, avocado, banana, and apple cider vinegar, are versatile and effective in home treatments.

A basic hair care routine should be personalized to meet the specific needs of each hair type. Washing, for example, should be done with appropriate natural shampoos, gently massaging the scalp to stimulate circulation and remove impurities. Conditioning is essential to hydrate and seal the cuticles, making it easier to detangle the strands. Natural hair masks, used weekly, offer deep hydration and nutrition, restoring hair vitality. Finishing with natural oils or creams helps protect the strands, control frizz, and style the hair.

Simple practices also make a difference in hair health. Avoiding heat tools or using them in moderation with adequate protection, rinsing hair with warm or cold water, and respecting the ideal washing frequency are habits that help preserve the strength and shine of the strands. By incorporating natural ingredients and adopting a conscious approach, it is possible to transform hair care into a moment of connection with yourself and with nature.

Understanding your hair type and needs is the first step in developing an effective routine that promotes health, beauty, and sustainability. Natural cosmetics, with their wealth of possibilities, offer the means to nourish the strands in a balanced and healthy way, reflecting the vitality and authenticity of each individual.

Hair, in its diversity and beauty, reveals both our individuality and the impact of the choices we make in daily care. Understanding its structure and needs allows us to address the specific challenges of each type of strand, creating routines that respect and celebrate its nature. This personalized attention, when combined with natural cosmetics, becomes an opportunity to nourish the hair with ingredients that not only meet its demands, but also promote sustainability and well-being.

In addition to applying appropriate products, it is essential to cultivate habits that preserve the integrity of the strands. Small changes, such as adjusting the water temperature during washing, protecting hair from the heat of tools, and adopting a balanced diet, have a significant impact on hair health. This daily care complements the use of natural ingredients, such as vegetable oils and plant extracts, which offer deep and lasting benefits while respecting the environment.

Caring for hair is a gesture that goes beyond aesthetics; it is a form of connection with oneself and with the natural world. By integrating conscious practices and pure ingredients into the hair routine, we transform this care into a moment of reconnection and celebration of our essence. Thus, each healthy and vibrant strand becomes a reflection of choices aligned with the harmony between body, mind, and nature.

# Chapter 6
# Sensitivity Test

The adoption of natural cosmetics is an increasingly popular choice among those seeking personal care aligned with healthier and more sustainable practices. This trend, however, requires careful and critical attention, as not all natural products are risk-free. Naturally derived ingredients, such as essential oils and plant extracts, can trigger adverse reactions, especially in people with sensitive skin or a predisposition to allergies. The idea that "natural" is synonymous with "safe" should be approached with caution, considering the individual particularities of each organism and the specific interactions that can occur between the skin and cosmetic components.

Performing a sensitivity test is a crucial step in avoiding discomfort and potentially serious complications. This procedure is not limited to preventing allergic reactions; it also serves as a preventive practice to establish a safer relationship with the products applied to the skin. The simplicity of the test does not diminish its importance: it is an effective way to assess how the skin reacts to specific substances, identifying possible irritations or sensitivities before the product is used on larger areas of the body. In addition, this step helps to build a more conscious care routine, respecting the unique needs of each person.

It is essential to understand that the skin, as the largest organ in the human body, plays a fundamental role in protection against external agents. However, its vulnerability to irritation and allergies reinforces the importance of taking preventive measures, especially in contexts that involve the application of new products. A well-executed sensitivity test reflects not only care for health, but also the appreciation of well-being and confidence when exploring the universe of natural cosmetics. In this way, it becomes possible to fully enjoy the benefits offered by the products, without compromising the safety or integrity of the skin.

Before using any cosmetic product, whether natural or industrialized, it is essential to perform a sensitivity test, a procedure that can prevent unwanted allergic reactions and ensure the safe and peaceful use of the products. This test, in addition to being simple and fast, is an essential practice for any skincare routine. It is especially recommended for those with sensitive skin or a history of allergies, being able to identify potential irritants before they affect larger areas of the body.

The main objective of the sensitivity test is to determine if your skin reacts adversely to the ingredients present in the chosen cosmetic. This includes even natural components, such as essential oils, plant extracts and clays, which, although natural, can cause reactions depending on individual sensitivity. Redness, itching, burning, swelling, rashes, flaking and dryness are among the most common symptoms of an allergic reaction. In extreme cases, there may be generalized swelling, difficulty breathing or even anaphylactic shock, which further reinforces the need to prevent these risks with a simple test.

To perform the sensitivity test, follow these steps carefully. First, choose a small, discreet area of the body, such as the inside of your forearm or behind your ear. This location should be easy to observe and not exposed to friction or other external agents that could interfere with the test. Then, wash the chosen area with mild soap and water, drying it gently to ensure that the skin is clean and free of any residue that could interfere with the evaluation.

With the skin prepared, apply a small amount of the product to the chosen area. Massage lightly to ensure that the product comes into direct contact with the skin. This contact should be maintained for a period of 24 to 48 hours, during which it is essential to avoid washing or rubbing the area. This wait is crucial to allow any reactions, even subtle ones, enough time to manifest.

At the end of the observation period, examine the area carefully. The absence of visible reactions, such as redness, itching, burning, swelling or any other abnormality, indicates a negative test, allowing safe use of the product. On the other hand, if there is any sign of irritation, the test is considered positive, and the product should not be used. In this case, wash the area immediately with mild soap and water and, if symptoms persist or worsen, seek medical advice or a dermatologist.

Testing should be accompanied by some additional practices to ensure greater safety. When a formulation contains multiple ingredients, it is ideal to test each component individually. Thus, if there is a reaction, it is possible to identify exactly which substance is responsible. Also, as skin sensitivity can change over time, it is prudent to repeat the test periodically, even if a product has been well tolerated on previous occasions.

Another point of attention is essential oils, known for their high concentration and potential to cause adverse reactions if used improperly. They should always be diluted in a carrier oil before use and subjected to a sensitivity test. This precaution is vital, as essential oils are often used in natural cosmetic treatments, but can be irritating even to skin that is not generally sensitive.

Finally, people with a history of allergies or particularly sensitive skin should seek medical advice before introducing new products into their skincare routine, even if they are of natural origin. A professional's opinion can offer valuable information about safe formulations and indicate personalized options, further reducing the risk of adverse reactions.

By performing a sensitivity test with due care, you can enjoy the benefits of natural cosmetics safely and consciously, ensuring that they contribute to the well-being and health of your skin. This simple procedure is an investment in safety and tranquility, promoting a harmonious and healthy relationship with the products we choose to take care of ourselves.

Integrating the sensitivity test into a care routine is a reflection of respect for the particularities of the skin and commitment to prevention. By adopting this practice, a safer and more effective path is created to explore the benefits of cosmetics, reducing the risks of negative experiences. More than just a protocol, it represents a stage of self-knowledge, allowing each person to better understand how their skin reacts to different substances, whether natural or synthetic.

Furthermore, awareness of potential irritants found even in the most harmless ingredients promotes a more informed approach to product choices. Personalization then becomes the key to building a care routine that not only respects skin health, but also values the diversity of individual needs. By combining science and precaution, it is possible to transform the act of caring for the skin into a moment of connection with one's own body.

With proper care, the universe of natural cosmetics ceases to be an unknown territory and becomes a reliable source of well-being. The sensitivity test is not just a preventive method, but a constant reminder that every gesture of care begins with safety and respect for our own characteristics. Thus, the search for healthy beauty becomes a genuine act of self-care and confidence.

# Chapter 7
# Natural Facial Cleansing

Facial cleansing is an indispensable practice to maintain the health and vitality of the skin, ensuring that it is always prepared to face the challenges of everyday life and to receive other treatments. This care goes far beyond aesthetics, playing an essential role in the protection and balance of the skin barrier. Impurities such as pollution particles, makeup residue and excess oil, when accumulated, can clog pores and trigger problems such as acne, irritation and premature aging. Therefore, adopting natural methods for facial cleansing not only protects the skin, but also reflects a commitment to more sustainable practices free of harsh chemical agents.

By opting for natural alternatives, respect for the skin's balance becomes a priority. Ingredients such as vegetable oils, clays and botanical extracts offer a unique combination of effective cleansing and gentleness, helping to maintain skin hydration and integrity. Each skin type, whether oily, dry, combination or sensitive, finds in these components options suited to its specific needs. For example, the astringent properties of clays and hydrolates are ideal for oily skin, while vegetable butters and soothing hydrolates offer comfort and nourishment for dry and sensitive skin. This customizable approach reinforces the effectiveness of natural products, which not only cleanse but deeply care for the skin.

Incorporating natural facial cleansing into your daily routine is more than just a functional choice; it is an opportunity to transform this moment into a self-care ritual. This process goes beyond simply removing waste, becoming a time to connect with your own body and renew yourself. Whether preparing a cleansing milk with nourishing oils or massaging your face with a refreshing aloe vera gel, each step offers benefits ranging from cell revitalization to improving skin texture and luminosity. Thus, natural facial cleansing not only contributes to a healthier appearance, but also promotes overall well-being.

Facial cleansing is an indispensable ritual to maintain the health and balance of the skin, providing benefits that go beyond aesthetics. Morning and night, this practice ensures the removal of accumulated impurities, such as makeup residue, pollution and oiliness, preventing problems such as clogged pores, acne and premature aging. More than that, cleansing promotes cell renewal, preparing the skin to better absorb nutrients from other products, such as moisturizers and serums, in addition to balancing pH and maintaining healthy bacterial flora.

Natural cosmetics offer effective and gentle alternatives, respecting the skin's balance and using ingredients that adapt to the specific needs of each skin type. Cleansing milks, natural soaps, refreshing gels and micellar waters are options that combine effectiveness with care. While cleansing milks and micellar waters offer hydration and softness, ideal for dry and sensitive skin, natural soaps with clays and cleansing gels with astringent extracts are perfect for oily and combination skin. Each choice provides specific care, allowing the skin to stay clean and healthy without harming its natural barrier.

The facial cleansing process begins with makeup removal, an essential step to prevent the accumulation of residue in the pores. Natural products like coconut oil or micellar water are effective and gentle options for this initial step. With makeup removed, the next step is to moisten your face with warm or cold water, which helps open pores and facilitates cleansing. The chosen product is then applied in gentle circular motions, stimulating circulation and ensuring even cleansing. After application, the face should be rinsed with warm or cold water to remove all of the product, and gently dried with a soft towel without rubbing.

For those who want to adopt totally natural methods, there are simple and effective recipes that can be prepared at home. Cleansing milk for dry skin is a nourishing and moisturizing option. To prepare it, mix 2 tablespoons of sweet almond vegetable oil with 1 tablespoon of shea butter, 2 tablespoons of rose hydrolate and 10 drops of lavender essential oil. Store the mixture in a dark glass bottle and apply with your hands or a cotton pad, massaging gently. Removal is done with warm or cold water, leaving the skin soft and hydrated.

For oily skin, a natural soap with green clay is an ideal choice. Start by melting 100g of vegetable glycerin base in a bain-marie. Add 1 tablespoon of green clay, 1 tablespoon of coconut vegetable oil and 10 drops of tea tree essential oil. Mix well and pour into a silicone mold. After 24 hours of drying, the soap will be ready to use, offering deep cleansing without drying out the skin.

For those with combination skin, a light and refreshing cleansing gel can be prepared with ½ cup aloe vera gel, 1 tablespoon witch hazel extract and 10 drops of lemon essential oil. Mix the ingredients in a container and store in a dark glass bottle. During application, gently massage the gel onto your face and rinse with warm or cold water. This method balances oiliness in the T-zone and keeps drier areas hydrated.

Regardless of skin type, choosing natural products and methods transforms your facial cleansing routine into a moment of self-care. This habit not only keeps the skin clean and healthy, but also promotes well-being and a greater connection with daily care. By incorporating these practices, you will be strengthening the natural balance of your skin and taking full advantage of the benefits of a more sustainable and conscious approach.

The continued use of natural methods for facial cleansing also encourages greater attention to the environmental impact of daily choices. Choosing biodegradable ingredients and recyclable packaging reinforces the commitment to sustainability, aligning personal care with environmental preservation. In addition, homemade production of products reduces dependence on industrial processes and contributes to a simpler and more conscious lifestyle, where each element used carries a clear purpose and respect for nature.

As these rituals become part of the routine, the skin responds not only with a healthier appearance, but with an overall feeling of balance and freshness. Regularity in practice, combined with attention to the specific needs of each season or moment of life, ensures that cleansing is always an act of harmony with the body. This sensitive and adaptable care reflects a deeper understanding of the connection between skin, well-being and the surrounding environment.

In this way, natural facial cleansing transcends its basic function, becoming a link between self-care and environmental responsibility. It is an invitation to slow down, dedicate time to yourself and recognize the value of conscious choices. Each step, from the selection of ingredients to the act of gently massaging the skin, symbolizes a journey of renewal and respect. Thus, the daily ritual not only nourishes the skin, but also strengthens the relationship with the world around us, creating a continuous cycle of care and balance.

# Chapter 8
# Facial Exfoliation

Facial exfoliation plays an essential role in maintaining the health and appearance of the skin, acting as a regenerative process that promotes cell renewal. By removing the surface layer of dead skin cells that naturally accumulates, this care not only reveals brighter and more even skin, but also prevents the appearance of problems such as acne, blackheads and enlarged pores. More than just a step in a skincare routine, exfoliation promotes a deep interaction between the skin and the products used, maximizing the absorption of active ingredients and enhancing the benefits of moisturizers, serums and other cosmetics.

One of the great benefits of exfoliation is its ability to stimulate blood circulation in the treated area, contributing to the oxygenation and nutrition of skin cells. This increase in blood flow not only improves the immediate appearance of the skin, giving it a healthy and vibrant look, but also acts in the long term, encouraging the production of collagen and elastin. These structural components are fundamental to maintain the firmness and elasticity of the skin, preventing signs of premature aging, such as wrinkles and fine lines. Thus, the regular practice of exfoliation becomes an ally in preventive and rejuvenating care.

Choosing the ideal exfoliation method is a critical aspect to ensure the best results without compromising skin health. Each skin type has its own peculiarities and responds differently to the stimuli provided by physical or chemical exfoliants. Sensitive skin, for example, can benefit from gentler natural ingredients like oats and honey, while oily skin can tolerate more intense exfoliation with clay or coffee. By respecting these differences and adopting practices that harmonize with individual needs, facial exfoliation ceases to be an isolated procedure and becomes an integral part of holistic and personalized care.

Facial exfoliation is essential care to keep skin healthy, even and radiant. It removes the surface layer of dead cells accumulated over time, revealing brighter, renewed skin. In addition, this practice promotes unclogging of pores, preventing blackheads and pimples, and contributes to a better use of the active ingredients present in other cosmetic products, such as moisturizers and serums, maximizing their effects.

Another important benefit of facial exfoliation is the stimulation of blood circulation. During the process, massage movements help increase the flow of oxygen and nutrients to skin cells, promoting a healthy and vibrant appearance. In the long term, this action can contribute to the production of collagen and elastin, proteins that support the firmness and elasticity of the skin, delaying the appearance of signs of aging, such as wrinkles and fine lines.

Choosing the most appropriate exfoliation method is essential to ensure effective results without harming skin health. Sensitive skin requires natural, gentle ingredients, such as oats and honey, while oily skin can tolerate more vigorous exfoliation with clay and coffee. Respecting the individual characteristics of each skin type is crucial to transform exfoliation into a safe step integrated into the care routine.

Among the benefits of exfoliation, cell renewal stands out, which leaves the skin more even and youthful. Unclogging pores prevents sebum buildup, reducing blackheads and pimples, while massage stimulates circulation, increasing skin oxygenation. In addition, the removal of dead cells improves the absorption of other cosmetic products, making treatments more effective. The ability of exfoliation to even out skin tone is also notable, contributing to the reduction of blemishes and marks.

There are two main methods of facial exfoliation: physical and chemical. Physical exfoliation uses solid particles, such as seeds and grains, to remove dead cells by friction. It is ideal for those who prefer a more natural and immediate method, and it is recommended to choose fine particles to avoid irritation. Chemical exfoliation uses substances such as acids and enzymes to promote controlled flaking, ideal for more resistant skin or specific treatments.

For each skin type, there is an appropriate method and frequency of exfoliation. Normal skin can opt for both physical and chemical exfoliation, performing the procedure once or twice a week. Dry skin benefits from gentle physical exfoliants or mild acids, such as lactic acid, applied weekly or every two weeks. Oily skin can tolerate more frequent exfoliation, twice a week, with larger particles or stronger acids, such as salicylic acid. Sensitive skin requires special care, with gentle exfoliants and a lower frequency, always observing the skin's reaction.

Preparing natural facial scrubs at home is a sustainable and personalized way to include this care in your routine. An oat and honey scrub, ideal for sensitive skin, is made with 2 tablespoons of finely ground rolled oats, 1 tablespoon of honey and 1 tablespoon of water. The mixture should be applied to damp skin, massaged gently and rinsed off with warm water. For dry skin, a sugar and coconut oil scrub combines 2 tablespoons of granulated sugar with 1 tablespoon of coconut oil, providing hydration and renewal.

Oily skin can rely on a coffee and green clay scrub, which combines 2 tablespoons of coffee grounds, 1 tablespoon of green clay and 1 tablespoon of water, offering deep cleansing and oil control. For combination skin, a grape seed and yogurt scrub is ideal: just mix 2 tablespoons of powdered grape seed with 1 tablespoon of plain yogurt, creating a nourishing paste that balances the different areas of the face.

To ensure effective and safe exfoliation, some practices must be followed. It is important to prepare the skin with prior cleansing, using products appropriate for your skin type. During application, the scrub should be massaged gently, avoiding excessive pressure and the delicate area around the eyes. After the procedure, rinse well with warm or cold water, removing all residues, and finish with a moisturizer to replenish lost hydration. As exfoliation makes the skin more sensitive to the sun, daily use of sunscreen is essential.

Respecting the indicated frequency for each skin type is essential to avoid irritation and sensitivity. Incorporating facial exfoliation properly into your routine provides healthier, more even and revitalized skin, transforming this care into a valuable ally for beauty and well-being.

The regular practice of facial exfoliation not only improves the appearance of the skin, but also promotes a moment of personal care that connects health and self-esteem. Incorporating this step into your weekly routine encourages greater attention to the specific needs of your skin, allowing for adjustments according to seasonal changes, age or lifestyle. This dynamic relationship with self-care strengthens the perception that healthy beauty is intrinsically linked to listening to one's own body and respecting its particularities.

By opting for natural or homemade scrubs, the ritual takes on an even more special meaning, highlighting the simplicity and effectiveness of accessible ingredients. Each application is a reminder of the transformative potential of sustainable practices, where conscious choices not only benefit the skin, but also promote a positive impact on the environment. Thus, the moment of exfoliation becomes more than just functional care: it transforms into a celebration of the balance between well-being and environmental responsibility.

With the proper frequency and choice of methods that respect skin integrity, facial exfoliation reinforces its relevance as an essential part of a skincare routine. It symbolizes not only the renewal of the skin, but also the renewal of a commitment to one's own health and vitality. Each movement, ingredient and result reflects a continuous investment in conscious beauty, marking the face not only with luminosity, but with the confidence of those who value self-care in a holistic way.

# Chapter 9
# Facial Hydration

Keeping skin properly hydrated is one of the most important fundamentals for preserving its health and vitality. Hydration not only promotes a more youthful and radiant appearance, but also plays a crucial role in the optimal functioning of the skin barrier, which acts as a natural defense against external aggressions. Factors such as pollution, climate variations and constant sun exposure can compromise this protection, resulting in dryness, irritation and even accelerated aging. Providing the skin with the necessary moisture helps to balance these daily challenges, ensuring that it remains resistant, soft and even.

The skin's ability to retain water is directly linked to its elasticity and luminosity. When properly hydrated, the skin becomes firmer and more flexible, reducing the appearance of wrinkles and fine lines. In addition, the natural glow that accompanies well-hydrated skin is not just aesthetic, but also an indicator of health and good circulation. By adopting natural moisturizers that contain ingredients such as aloe vera, vegetable butters or hyaluronic acid of plant origin, it is possible to nourish the skin effectively and sustainably, promoting deep hydration without the use of harmful synthetic compounds.

Integrating hydration practices into your daily routine is a valuable investment in skin care. Applying moisturizer right after cleansing and at times of specific need maximizes the benefits of the product, as clean, slightly damp skin absorbs nutrients and moisturizing components better. Furthermore, complementing this routine with a good intake of water creates a powerful synergy that keeps the skin nourished from the inside out. By valuing hydration as a priority, not only is skin health reinforced, but also its ability to face external challenges with greater resistance and resilience.

Keeping skin properly hydrated is essential to preserve its health, beauty and functionality. Hydration plays a vital role in the integrity of the skin barrier, the first line of defense against external factors such as pollution, microorganisms and sun exposure. When this barrier is compromised, the skin loses its ability to retain water, becoming more vulnerable to dryness, irritation and even premature aging. By providing the necessary moisture, we reinforce its natural resistance, ensuring soft, supple and even skin.

Skin elasticity is directly linked to hydration levels. Well-hydrated skin is firmer and more resistant, reducing the appearance of wrinkles and fine lines. In addition, its ability to reflect light evenly gives it a natural, healthy glow, an indicator of good circulation and cell nutrition. Adopting natural moisturizers based on ingredients such as aloe vera, vegetable butters and plant-derived hyaluronic acid not only deeply nourishes the skin, but also eliminates the need for synthetic compounds, promoting more sustainable and healthy care.

The habit of moisturizing the skin regularly is essential. Applying moisturizer after cleansing, when the skin is clean and slightly damp, increases the absorption of active ingredients and enhances the benefits of the product. In addition, internal hydration, obtained through good water intake, complements external care, creating a balance that keeps the skin nourished and prepared to face daily challenges.

The daily facial hydration routine has numerous benefits. It helps maintain the integrity of the skin barrier, preventing water loss and protecting against external aggressions. It also relieves dryness, reducing flaking and tightness. Skin elasticity is improved, which helps prevent the appearance of signs of aging. Well-hydrated skin reflects light evenly, promoting a luminous and healthy appearance, in addition to smoothing its texture, making it softer and more even.

Natural moisturizers are excellent allies for all skin types, offering options adapted to the specific needs of each. Vegetable oils, such as coconut, argan, jojoba and rosehip, are rich in fatty acids and antioxidants, providing deep hydration. Vegetable butters, such as shea, cocoa and mango, have a creamy texture and offer intense hydration, being ideal for dry and parched skin. Aloe vera, with its soothing and healing properties, is perfect for sensitive skin, while plant-derived hyaluronic acid attracts and retains water, promoting long-lasting hydration and filling in fine lines.

Choosing the right moisturizer depends on your skin type. Normal skin can opt for light, fluid moisturizers, while dry skin benefits from creamier, more nourishing textures. Oily skin requires oil-free formulas, usually in gel or lotion, to avoid excess oil. For combination skin, moisturizers that balance the different needs of the T-zone and drier areas are ideal. Sensitive skin needs hypoallergenic formulas, free of fragrances and dyes, with soothing ingredients like chamomile and calendula.

Preparing natural moisturizers at home is a practical and personalized alternative. For dry skin, a moisturizer can be made with 1 tablespoon of shea butter, 1 tablespoon of rosehip oil, 1 tablespoon of rose hydrosol and 5 drops of lavender essential oil. Melt the shea butter in a bain-marie, mix the other ingredients and store in a dark bottle. Apply to clean face, massaging gently until absorbed.

For oily skin, mix ½ cup aloe vera gel, 1 tablespoon jojoba oil and 10 drops of tea tree essential oil. This combination hydrates without weighing it down and helps control oiliness. For combination skin, combine 1 tablespoon of jojoba oil, 1 tablespoon of aloe vera gel and 1 tablespoon of geranium hydrosol. This blend promotes balanced and healthy hydration.

Following a few simple practices enhances the results of facial hydration. Always cleanse the skin before applying moisturizer to ensure pores are free of impurities. Applying moisturizer to damp skin helps retain water, while massaging during application stimulates blood circulation. In addition, internal hydration through good water intake is essential. Protecting the skin with sunscreen daily complements care, preventing water loss and damage caused by UV rays.

By incorporating facial hydration into your routine, you are investing in healthier, younger and more resistant skin. With the right choices and consistent habits, it is possible to provide the skin with everything it needs to stay radiant, luscious and well protected against the challenges of everyday life.

Hydrating the skin goes beyond aesthetic care; it is an essential gesture of preservation and strengthening. Each application of a good moisturizer acts as a shield, protecting the skin from daily aggressions while reinforcing its natural ability to regenerate. This continuous care is especially relevant in a world where pollution and climate change constantly challenge skin health, demanding attention and products that deliver more than just a superficial effect.

Personalization is one of the greatest advantages of facial hydration, allowing each skin type to receive exactly what it needs. From rich, nourishing formulas for dry skin to light gels that balance oiliness, the possibilities are wide and versatile. With natural ingredients, such as butters, vegetable oils and aloe vera, each product becomes a solution that not only cares, but respects the nature of the skin and the environment. These ingredients act as allies, nourishing deeply while offering a unique and invigorating sensory experience.

When hydration becomes a daily habit, the face clearly reflects the benefits: softness, luminosity and resilience. It is not just the skin that is renewed; the act of taking care of yourself strengthens self-esteem and creates a routine of well-being that transcends the physical. Each layer of moisturizer applied is a reaffirmation of the commitment to one's own body, translating into skin that, in addition to being healthy, exudes vitality and balance in all phases of life.

# Chapter 10
# Natural Facial Masks

Natural facial masks are a powerful and accessible solution to enhance skincare. Formulated with pure ingredients extracted directly from nature, they offer a wide range of benefits from hydration and nourishment to purification and rejuvenation. In addition to promoting visible results in the short term, these intensive treatments value the natural balance of the skin, minimizing the use of harsh chemicals. Incorporating natural masks into your skincare routine is a way to combine well-being, aesthetics, and sustainability in a single gesture.

When applying a facial mask, the skin receives a high concentration of active ingredients that penetrate deeply, promoting significant changes in its texture, luminosity, and vitality. Ingredients such as clays, fruits, vegetable oils, and hydrolates are rich in essential nutrients, vitamins, and antioxidants that help restore skin health. For example, moisturizing masks based on avocado and honey are ideal for dry skin, while green clay masks help control oiliness and purify pores. This variety allows you to customize care according to individual needs, ensuring effective and targeted results.

In addition to the direct benefits for the skin, the use of facial masks provides a moment of relaxation and self-care. This ritual can be transformed into a complete sensory experience, combining natural aromas and a break from the routine to promote emotional well-being. Regular application, once or twice a week, complements daily care and helps to create a deeper connection with the body's needs. By exploring different combinations of ingredients and textures, it is possible to discover which natural masks best meet the particularities of the skin, promoting complete, healthy, and truly transformative care.

Natural facial masks are a powerful resource to intensify skincare, bringing together benefits ranging from hydration and nutrition to purification and rejuvenation. Formulated with pure and accessible ingredients, these masks provide quick and visible results while respecting the natural balance of the skin. Incorporating them into your skincare routine is a simple way to combine well-being, beauty, and sustainability, valuing practices that prioritize skin health and the use of natural substances.

When applied, the masks offer a concentrated dose of active ingredients that penetrate deeply into the skin, promoting noticeable changes in texture, luminosity, and vitality. Ingredients such as clays, vegetable oils, fruits, and hydrolates are rich in vitamins, minerals, and antioxidants essential for restoring skin health. For example, a mask based on avocado and honey is ideal for dry skin, offering intense hydration, while green clay is recommended for oily skin, helping to control oiliness and purify pores. The diversity of combinations allows you to customize care, meeting the unique needs of each skin type.

In addition to the benefits for the skin, facial masks become moments of relaxation and self-care. During the application time, it is possible to create a unique sensory experience, taking advantage of the natural aromas of the ingredients and allowing a break from the daily routine. This ritual, which can be performed once or twice a week, complements regular care and strengthens the connection with one's own body. Experimenting with different masks and discovering those that best meet the needs of the skin is a path to achieving more complete and transformative care.

Facial masks offer various benefits, from deep hydration and nutrition to purification and revitalization of the skin. They treat intensively, concentrating active ingredients that provide quick results, such as softness, luminosity, and uniformity. Purifying masks with clays, for example, unclog pores, control excess oil, and prevent blackheads and pimples. The calming versions, with aloe vera or chamomile, relieve irritation and reduce redness. In addition, rejuvenating masks with antioxidant ingredients, such as rosehip oil or vitamin C, help prevent the signs of aging, giving a youthful and radiant appearance.

Choosing the ideal facial mask is essential to ensure the best results. Normal skin can use moisturizing and nourishing masks to maintain balance, while dry skin benefits from richer masks with vegetable oils and butters. For oily skin, purifying and astringent masks with clays or activated charcoal are ideal. Combination skin requires combinations that meet the different areas of the face, and sensitive skin should prioritize calming formulas, without fragrances or dyes.

Creating natural masks at home is a practical and economical way to personalize care. A moisturizing avocado and honey mask, for example, is prepared with ½ mashed ripe avocado and 1 tablespoon of honey. The mixture should be applied to clean, dry skin, remaining for 15 to 20 minutes before being rinsed off with warm water. For purification, a green clay mask combines 2 tablespoons of clay powder with water or hydrolate to form a creamy paste. After application, leave it on for the same period and remove with warm water. Calming masks, such as aloe vera and chamomile, mix 2 tablespoons of aloe vera gel with 1 tablespoon of concentrated chamomile tea, offering immediate relief for sensitive skin.

When applying facial masks, some care enhances the results. First of all, it is essential to clean the skin well to remove impurities and prepare the face to receive the active ingredients of the mask. The application should be done in uniform layers, avoiding the sensitive area of the eyes and lips. During the application time, relaxing and enjoying the moment helps transform care into a wellness ritual. After complete removal of the mask, it is recommended to finish with a moisturizer to prolong the effects and replenish hydration.

The ideal frequency for using masks varies according to the individual needs of the skin. Generally, it is recommended to apply them once or twice a week, adjusting the frequency according to the skin's response. This simple habit complements daily care and provides healthier, more beautiful, and revitalized skin.

Natural facial masks are an excellent way to intensify skincare, offering specific treatments for different types and needs. Incorporating them into your routine is a significant step towards achieving healthier, more balanced, and radiant skin while enjoying precious moments of self-care and relaxation.

The regular use of natural facial masks transcends aesthetic care, transforming into a holistic practice that benefits both the skin and emotional well-being. Each application is not just an intensive treatment, but also a moment of pause, where the body and mind find relief from the fast pace of everyday life. Incorporating this ritual into your weekly routine allows you to not only achieve visible results but also cultivate a deeper connection with your own needs.

The versatility of natural masks allows for customization that meets different skin types and specific demands. Whether to hydrate, purify, or rejuvenate, these treatments value the simple and powerful ingredients that nature offers, ensuring safe and effective results. This conscious and sustainable approach reinforces the commitment to integral care, promoting a relationship of respect for both the body and the environment.

By exploring different combinations and textures, the facial mask routine becomes an act of discovery and self-care. Each homemade preparation or application reflects a moment of personal dedication, where beauty is nurtured from the inside out. Thus, in addition to more radiant and healthy skin, the benefits include a sense of balance and renewal that lasts long beyond the minutes dedicated to this ritual.

# Chapter 11
# Natural Facial Toner

Skin toning is an indispensable step to enhance facial care, promoting essential balance after cleansing and exfoliation. This process goes beyond simply removing remaining residue: it acts as a multifunctional ally that revitalizes, refreshes, and prepares the skin to receive subsequent treatments. Natural facial toner plays a central role in this context, offering benefits ranging from harmonizing skin pH to preventing excess oil and reducing the appearance of dilated pores. Thus, its regular use translates into healthier, firmer, and more luminous skin, highlighting the importance of its inclusion in any skincare routine.

The ability of natural toner to balance the skin's pH is one of its most notable aspects. After cleansing, the skin may present a slight imbalance that, if not corrected, can compromise its natural protective barrier, leaving it vulnerable to external aggressions. With its slightly acidic composition, the toner helps restore this balance, strengthening the skin barrier and maintaining healthy bacterial flora. In addition, its calming and refreshing action is immediate relief for sensitive skin, offering comfort and reducing irritation and redness, which makes it an especially effective product for sensitive or reactive skin.

By enhancing the absorption of subsequently applied products, natural toner takes on a strategic role in the skincare routine. It creates an ideal base for moisturizers, serums, and other treatments to penetrate deeper into the skin, maximizing their benefits. This characteristic, combined with the toning and revitalizing action, promotes a rejuvenated appearance, with a uniform texture and soft touch. Thus, the use of natural facial toners, rich in plant extracts and carefully selected ingredients, not only optimizes daily care but also contributes to visibly more balanced and radiant skin.

Skin toning is an indispensable step to enhance facial care, promoting essential balance after cleansing and exfoliation. This process goes beyond simply removing remaining residue: it acts as a multifunctional ally that revitalizes, refreshes, and prepares the skin to receive subsequent treatments. Natural facial toner plays a central role in this context, offering benefits ranging from harmonizing skin pH to preventing excess oil and reducing the appearance of dilated pores. Thus, its regular use translates into healthier, firmer, and more luminous skin, highlighting the importance of its inclusion in any skincare routine.

The ability of natural toner to balance the skin's pH is one of its most notable aspects. After cleansing, the skin may present a slight imbalance that, if not corrected, can compromise its natural protective barrier, leaving it vulnerable to external aggressions. With its slightly acidic composition, the toner helps restore this balance, strengthening the skin barrier and maintaining healthy bacterial flora. In addition, its calming and refreshing action is immediate relief for sensitive skin, offering comfort and reducing irritation and redness, which makes it an especially effective product for sensitive or reactive skin.

By enhancing the absorption of subsequently applied products, natural toner takes on a strategic role in the skincare routine. It creates an ideal base for moisturizers, serums, and other treatments to penetrate deeper into the skin, maximizing their benefits. This characteristic, combined with the toning and revitalizing action, promotes a rejuvenated appearance, with a uniform texture and soft touch. Thus, the use of natural facial toners, rich in plant extracts and carefully selected ingredients, not only optimizes daily care but also contributes to visibly more balanced and radiant skin.

The benefits of natural facial toner are wide-ranging and cover various dimensions of skincare. One of its main attributes is to complement cleansing, removing the last residues of impurities, makeup, and products that may remain on the skin even after washing. This ensures a feeling of purity and prepares the skin surface for the following steps. In addition, it is an invaluable ally in restoring the skin's natural pH. After cleansing, the natural acidity can be temporarily affected, but the toner, with its slightly acidic pH, helps to correct this change, promoting the maintenance of a balanced microbiota that protects against harmful external agents.

Another notable point is the comfort that the toner provides, especially for more sensitive skin. Soothing and refreshing ingredients, such as plant extracts and hydrolates, act to soothe irritation, reducing redness and inflammation. This effect is particularly beneficial for those dealing with conditions of heightened sensitivity, creating a feeling of freshness that helps revitalize the skin.

Preparing the skin for subsequent care is another essential function of the facial toner. By removing any residual barrier, it favors the absorption of products such as moisturizers and serums, optimizing their effects. Thus, the skin not only receives the necessary nutrients but also gains a firmer, more uniform, and healthier appearance, highlighting the toning and revitalizing action of the product. In specific cases, such as oily skin, the toner can also play an astringent role, controlling oiliness, especially in the T-zone, and contributing to the prevention of acne and excessive shine.

Different types of natural facial toners are formulated to meet various skin needs. Moisturizers, for example, are rich in ingredients such as rose hydrolate and aloe vera, promoting hydration and softness. Astringent toners, made with witch hazel hydrolate and tea tree essential oil, offer an effective solution for controlling oiliness and dilated pores. For those looking to soothe irritation, soothing toners with chamomile hydrolate and calendula extract provide gentle care. Finally, revitalizing toners, composed of vitamin C and cucumber extract, give the skin a renewed glow and a rejuvenated appearance.

The choice of the ideal toner should be based on the skin type and its specific characteristics. For normal skin, it is interesting to opt for moisturizing and revitalizing products, maintaining the natural balance. Dry skin, in turn, benefits from toners with high moisturizing power, while oily skin finds astringents to be the solution to minimize oiliness and dilated pores. Those with combination skin can explore formulas that act both in controlling oiliness and hydration. For sensitive skin, it is essential to prioritize soothing toners, formulated with mild ingredients and free of fragrances, to avoid adverse reactions.

Natural facial toner recipes are a practical and economical way to integrate this care into your routine. For example, a rose moisturizing toner can be prepared simply by storing 100 ml of rose hydrolate in a dark glass bottle with a spray bottle, ready to be applied to clean, dry skin. For those looking for an astringent effect, the mixture of 100 ml of witch hazel hydrolate with 10 drops of tea tree essential oil is an effective combination, stored in the same way. A soothing toner, in turn, can be made by combining 100 ml of chamomile hydrolate with a tablespoon of calendula extract, promoting immediate relief and comfort for irritated skin.

The correct application of the facial toner also enhances its benefits. It should be used after cleansing and exfoliation when the skin is most receptive. Whether with a cotton pad or spray bottle, the product should be distributed evenly, always avoiding the sensitive eye area. And, unlike other products, the toner does not need to be rinsed off, allowing its active ingredients to be fully absorbed before applying moisturizer.

Incorporating natural facial toner into your daily routine is a strategic choice for those seeking balanced and radiant skin. Through natural ingredients and a conscious approach, it is possible to achieve results that promote not only beauty but also health and well-being for the skin in the long term.

The practice of integrating natural facial toner into everyday life reflects conscious care connected to the individual needs of the skin. Each application is an opportunity to restore the harmony of the epidermis, reinforcing its natural defenses and providing a moment of renewal. This simple but significant gesture strengthens the relationship with personal care, transforming a routine into a ritual of self-care and appreciation of well-being.

The benefits of facial toner go beyond the visible, as its natural composition also reduces exposure to harsh chemicals present in many conventional cosmetics. Thus, by opting for formulas based on plant extracts, hydrolates, and essential oils, we promote not only skin health but also a positive impact on the environment. The choice of natural ingredients is a reflection of a sustainable approach that benefits both the skin and the planet.

Finally, natural facial toner stands out as an essential piece in the mosaic of skincare, uniting functionality, simplicity, and effectiveness. Its versatility and wide range of benefits make it an indispensable ally, regardless of skin type or condition. Incorporating it into your routine is ensuring that each stage of care is enhanced, reflecting in balanced, revitalized, and vibrant skin.

# Chapter 12
# Dark Circles and Bags

The area around the eyes is especially vulnerable to the effects of time, external conditions, and daily habits, requiring specific care to preserve its healthy appearance and minimize unwanted signs, such as dark circles and bags. These signs are often the result of factors such as tiredness, genetic predisposition, aging, or even lifestyle imbalances. Although common, they can be mitigated through simple and consistent practices, combined with natural ingredients that soothe, revitalize, and decongest this sensitive area. Proper attention to these aspects not only improves appearance, but also contributes to a more rested and confident countenance.

Dark circles, characterized by the darkened tone around the eyes, often reflect the interaction of visible blood vessels under the thin skin or hyperpigmentation triggered by sun exposure or aging. Bags, manifested as swelling under the eyes, often result from fluid retention, reduced skin elasticity, or inflammation. Despite their multifactorial causes, both dark circles and bags can be treated with accessible methods, such as cold compresses, gentle massages, and natural formulas that combine vegetable oils, botanical extracts, and antioxidants. These elements help to improve local circulation, reduce inflammation, and deeply nourish the skin.

Adopting habits that promote the balance of the body is also essential to take care of this delicate area. Good hydration, restful nights of sleep, and a nutrient-rich diet are pillars to prevent and minimize these signs. On the other hand, protection against solar radiation and the reduction of the consumption of substances such as alcohol and caffeine complement these measures, avoiding factors that accentuate the wear and tear of the skin around the eyes. In this way, regular and conscious care, combined with the use of natural alternatives, transforms the approach to treating dark circles and bags into an effective and restorative routine, promoting a renewed and vibrant look.

The area around the eyes is especially vulnerable to the effects of time, external conditions, and daily habits, requiring specific care to preserve its healthy appearance and minimize unwanted signs, such as dark circles and bags. These signs are often the result of factors such as tiredness, genetic predisposition, aging, or even lifestyle imbalances. Although common, they can be mitigated through simple and consistent practices, combined with natural ingredients that soothe, revitalize, and decongest this sensitive area. Proper attention to these aspects not only improves appearance, but also contributes to a more rested and confident countenance.

Dark circles, characterized by the darkened tone around the eyes, often reflect the interaction of visible blood vessels under the thin skin or hyperpigmentation triggered by sun exposure or aging. Bags, manifested as swelling under the eyes, often result from fluid retention, reduced skin elasticity, or inflammation. Despite their multifactorial causes, both dark circles and bags can be treated with accessible methods, such as cold compresses, gentle massages, and natural formulas that combine vegetable oils, botanical extracts, and antioxidants. These elements help to improve local circulation, reduce inflammation, and deeply nourish the skin.

The origin of dark circles and bags is quite diverse and depends on factors such as genetics, lifestyle, and overall health. In the case of dark circles, their coloration can vary from purplish to brownish tones, depending on the thickness of the skin and the presence of blood vessels or pigmentation. In people with a genetic predisposition, the skin around the eyes is thinner and more transparent, making blood vessels more visible and creating a darkened appearance. Tiredness, poor sleep, and stress impair blood circulation in the area, facilitating the accumulation of fluids and toxins that accentuate these signs.

Bags, on the other hand, are often associated with fluid retention or loss of skin elasticity, which becomes more evident with age. Excessive sun exposure without protection can aggravate both dark circles and bags, stimulating melanin production and leading to the appearance of spots. In addition, inadequate eating habits, such as excessive consumption of sodium and processed foods, contribute significantly to swelling in the region, as do allergies, which can cause local inflammation.

Adopting specific care for the skin around the eyes is essential to deal with these problems. Gentle cleansing is the first step, as it removes residue and makeup without harming the skin. Delicate products, such as micellar water or jojoba vegetable oil, are ideal for this sensitive area. Hydration also plays a crucial role, and the use of specific eye creams, with light textures and nourishing ingredients, helps maintain skin elasticity and radiance.

In addition, sun protection should not be neglected. Applying sunscreens formulated for the eye area protects the skin from UV radiation and prevents premature aging. Another simple and effective care is gentle massage in the region, which stimulates blood circulation and lymphatic drainage, reducing swelling. Cold compresses, such as cucumber slices or chilled chamomile tea, are great for soothing the skin and reducing inflammation.

Natural recipes offer practical and economical solutions to treat dark circles and bags. For example, a rosehip and chamomile cream combines moisturizing and soothing properties. To prepare it, simply melt half a teaspoon of beeswax in a bain-marie and mix it with a tablespoon of rosehip oil and chamomile hydrosol. The cream should be stored in a small, clean container and applied at night, with gentle circular motions.

Green tea compresses are another effective option. Green tea, known for its antioxidant and decongestant properties, helps reduce swelling and dark circles. To use it, simply prepare the tea, let it cool, and apply the sachets over closed eyes for about 15 minutes. A cucumber and potato mask combines the soothing and refreshing properties of these ingredients. The mixture is made by grating half a cucumber and half a raw potato, applying the paste directly over closed eyes.

Some daily practices can be incorporated to prevent and treat these signs. Sleeping between 7 and 8 hours a night is essential to avoid tiredness and stress that aggravate dark circles and bags. A balanced diet, rich in vitamins and minerals, promotes skin health and reduces fluid retention. Moderate consumption of alcohol and caffeine is also important, as both substances can dehydrate the body and intensify problems.

Drinking plenty of water is another essential measure, as it helps eliminate toxins and keeps the skin hydrated. During sleep, elevating your head with an extra pillow can prevent fluid buildup in the eye area. In addition, the use of sunglasses with UV protection protects the skin around the eyes from sun damage.

When home care is not enough to significantly reduce dark circles and bags, it is advisable to seek the guidance of a doctor or dermatologist. In cases where these signs persist, they may be related to underlying health conditions, such as anemia or kidney problems, which require specialized treatment.

Taking care of the eye area is a gesture that goes beyond aesthetics, promoting health and well-being. Adopting daily practices that involve gentle cleansing, proper hydration, sun protection, and the use of natural treatments not only minimizes signs of tiredness, but also strengthens the delicate skin in this region. With consistency and attention to detail, it is possible to restore the freshness of the look and promote a lighter and more rejuvenated appearance.

Attention to the eye area is not limited to combating dark circles and bags, but also involves building a relationship of continuous care with this delicate area. Each gesture, whether applying a cream or performing a gentle massage, is an opportunity to strengthen the connection with one's own body and cultivate habits that directly reflect on appearance and overall well-being. Thus, in addition to visible results, there is a gain in confidence and a sense of self-care that transcends aesthetic benefits.

Investing in natural solutions and simple practices not only enhances results, but also rescues the simplicity of personal care rituals. Ingredients such as green tea, cucumber, and rosehip reveal the power of accessible and sustainable elements, promoting skin health while minimizing environmental impacts. This balance between effectiveness and respect for the environment is an invitation to reflect on the conscious choice of products and methods that integrate health and sustainability.

As you build a routine focused on the eye area, it becomes clear that consistency and respect for the skin's needs are pillars to achieve lasting results. A revitalized and luminous look is not only a reflection of the techniques and products applied, but also of a continuous dedication that values the integral care of the body. This path of attention and affection transforms the approach to daily care into a celebration of one's own essence, with the promise of a renewed and vibrant countenance.

# Chapter 13
# Acne Naturally

Acne is a common skin manifestation that reflects a set of interconnected internal and external factors, significantly influencing the appearance and emotional health of those who face it. Although often associated with adolescence, this condition can occur at any stage of life, being marked by lesions such as blackheads, pimples and, in the most severe cases, nodules and cysts. These signs result from a combination of hormonal imbalances, excess oil, clogged pores, and the action of bacteria that proliferate in conducive environments. In addition to representing an aesthetic discomfort, acne can be aggravated by inadequate practices, making a careful and effective approach essential.

Acne skin care begins with proper cleansing, which should be done with gentle products, capable of removing impurities without causing dryness or irritation. Periodic exfoliation also plays a vital role, helping to prevent clogged pores, as long as it is done in moderation to avoid further inflammation. In addition, toning with natural formulas that soothe and balance sebum production complements the routine, while moisturizing, with light and oil-free products, preserves the skin's protective barrier. Regular use of sunscreen is equally crucial, as exposure to UV rays can intensify inflammation and cause blemishes, making treatment even more challenging.

The integration of natural solutions enhances acne skin care, taking advantage of the therapeutic properties of ingredients such as green clay, tea tree essential oil, and aloe vera. These components offer a combined action against excessive oiliness, inflammation and bacterial proliferation, promoting effective and less aggressive treatment. In addition, lifestyle changes, such as maintaining a balanced diet, rich in antioxidants and low in inflammatory foods, combined with adequate water intake, play an essential complementary role. Thus, a comprehensive plan that combines natural cosmetics, healthy habits and dermatological monitoring ensures healthier skin and a significant improvement in the visual and emotional aspects of acne.

Acne is a common skin manifestation that reflects a set of interconnected internal and external factors, significantly influencing the appearance and emotional health of those who face it. Although often associated with adolescence, this condition can occur at any stage of life, being marked by lesions such as blackheads, pimples and, in the most severe cases, nodules and cysts. These signs result from a combination of hormonal imbalances, excess oil, clogged pores, and the action of bacteria that proliferate in conducive environments. In addition to representing an aesthetic discomfort, acne can be aggravated by inadequate practices, making a careful and effective approach essential.

Acne skin care begins with proper cleansing, which should be done with gentle products, capable of removing impurities without causing dryness or irritation. Periodic exfoliation also plays a vital role, helping to prevent clogged pores, as long as it is done in moderation to avoid further inflammation. In addition, toning with natural formulas that soothe and balance sebum production complements the routine, while moisturizing, with light and oil-free products, preserves the skin's protective barrier. Regular use of sunscreen is equally crucial, as exposure to UV rays can intensify inflammation and cause blemishes, making treatment even more challenging.

Although there are countless conventional treatments for acne, natural cosmetics offer a gentler and more effective approach, taking advantage of the potential of ingredients with therapeutic properties. Acne, which arises from processes such as inflammation of the sebaceous glands and hair follicles, has well-defined causes that, when understood, allow for more targeted treatments.

One of the main causes of acne is excess oil, which can be triggered by hormonal changes, genetic predisposition, and environmental factors. This excess sebum creates an environment conducive to the proliferation of bacteria, such as Propionibacterium acnes (P. acnes), which is naturally present on the skin. When pores are clogged by the accumulation of dead cells and impurities, this bacterium finds an ideal environment to grow, triggering inflammation and the characteristic lesions of acne, such as pimples and blackheads.

The different types of acne vary in severity. Comedonal acne is marked by blackheads, which can be open (blackheads) or closed (whiteheads). Papulopustular acne includes reddish papules and pustules containing pus, indicating more intense inflammation. In the most severe cases, nodulocystic acne presents large, painful nodules and deep lesions, requiring more specialized care.

Caring for acne-prone skin requires a specific routine, starting with gentle cleansing. Washing your face twice a day, morning and night, with a product specifically for acne-prone skin helps remove excess oil without drying or irritating the skin. Exfoliation, performed once or twice a week, is essential to unclog pores, but should be done in moderation to avoid aggravating inflammation. Natural ingredients such as oats, which have soothing properties, can be incorporated to exfoliate effectively and gently.

After cleansing, toning is essential. An astringent toner formulated with ingredients such as witch hazel hydrosol and tea tree essential oil helps control oiliness and reduce the appearance of pores. In addition, hydration is a crucial step, even for oily skin. Oil-free moisturizers, with a light texture, help preserve the skin barrier without clogging pores.

Sun protection is an often overlooked but fundamental aspect of acne management. Sun exposure can exacerbate inflammation and leave blemishes that are difficult to treat. Using a lightweight sunscreen specifically for acne-prone skin daily is a way to prevent further damage.

In addition to topical care, diet plays an important role. Eating a diet rich in fruits, vegetables and anti-inflammatory foods, while avoiding processed products and those rich in sugars and fats, helps improve skin health. Adequate water intake also helps eliminate toxins, while avoiding excessive consumption of dairy products and foods with a high glycemic index can reduce acne breakouts.

Natural acne care recipes offer affordable and effective solutions. A green clay face mask, for example, is simple to prepare. Simply mix two tablespoons of green clay powder with filtered water or witch hazel hydrosol until it forms a creamy paste. Applied to a clean, dry face, the mask should act for 15 to 20 minutes before being removed with warm water. Green clay, with its purifying and anti-inflammatory properties, helps control oiliness and reduce acne lesions.

Another practical solution is the tea tree facial tonic. Mix 100 ml of witch hazel hydrosol with 10 drops of tea tree essential oil and store in a dark glass bottle with a spray bottle. Applied after cleansing, this tonic helps fight bacteria and soothe inflammation. For spot care, tea tree drying gel is ideal. Mix a tablespoon of aloe vera gel with two drops of tea tree essential oil and apply directly to pimples before bed. Aloe vera, with its healing action, complements the antibacterial efficacy of the essential oil.

Incorporating a natural oat and honey scrub is also a practical and nourishing option for the skin. Mix two tablespoons of finely ground rolled oats with one tablespoon of honey until you get a paste. Gently massage onto damp face and rinse with warm water. Oats remove dead skin cells while soothing the skin, and honey provides hydration and antibacterial properties.

A comprehensive approach that includes topical care, lifestyle changes, and the use of natural cosmetics can transform the way acne is treated. The commitment to a consistent routine adapted to individual needs results in a more balanced, healthy and acne-free skin, promoting not only an aesthetic improvement, but also emotional, with greater confidence and well-being.

The search for natural solutions for acne transcends the simple concern with appearance, connecting care practices to the appreciation of health and the overall balance of the body. The combination of botanical ingredients and lifestyle changes reaffirms the power of nature as an ally in promoting healthy skin and reducing acne lesions. In addition, this approach encourages self-knowledge and patience, remembering that visible results arise from persistence and respect for one's own rhythm of healing.

The management of acne with natural cosmetics also opens space for the rediscovery of simple but effective rituals, such as the application of clay masks and the use of homemade tonics. These moments of self-care have the potential to transform the relationship with the skin, establishing a routine that not only treats, but also prevents future challenges. This harmony between what is applied externally and internal changes, such as diet and hydration, highlights how much integrated care can positively impact skin health.

Finally, the path to acne-free skin is not just about eliminating imperfections, but also about cultivating habits that reflect overall well-being. By integrating knowledge about the benefits of nature with a broad and careful view of the body, it is possible to achieve balanced skin and a more confident relationship with one's own image. This process, in addition to restoring skin health, reinforces the value of conscious practices that celebrate individuality and self-respect.

# Chapter 14
# Skin Spots

Skin spots are a common challenge for many people, reflecting changes in pigmentation that can vary in intensity and origin. These changes, often associated with sun exposure, aging, inflammatory processes, or hormonal changes, affect the evenness of skin tone and, in some cases, directly influence self-esteem. As diverse as their causes may be, the correct approach can significantly reduce their appearance, promoting a more even, luminous, and healthy complexion. Natural cosmetics offer gentle and effective alternatives, exploring the benefits of ingredients such as clay, vegetable oils, and antioxidants, which lighten and revitalize without harming the skin.

Prevention is the first step in caring for spots, with daily sun protection being one of the most important strategies. Exposure to UV rays, even on cloudy days, is the main cause of increased melanin production, the pigment that, when accumulated irregularly, gives rise to spots. In addition, habits such as avoiding the sun during peak hours and wearing hats and clothing that block ultraviolet radiation complement topical protection. At the same time, adopting a diet rich in antioxidants, such as vitamins C and E, strengthens the skin from the inside out, helping to fight free radicals that accelerate aging and promote hyperpigmentation.

An even skin tone can be achieved with the use of natural treatments that have regenerating and lightening properties. Ingredients such as white clay, known for its smoothing and illuminating effect, and rosehip oil, a powerful cell regenerator, are potent allies against different types of spots, such as acne, melasma, and age spots. By integrating these treatments into a care routine that includes proper cleansing, balanced hydration, and the use of sunscreen, it is possible to gradually reduce the appearance of spots and prevent the appearance of new ones. This holistic approach, combining protection, nutrition, and targeted treatment, provides effective and long-lasting results, promoting visibly more even and revitalized skin.

Skin spots are a common challenge for many people, reflecting changes in pigmentation that can vary in intensity and origin. These changes, often associated with sun exposure, aging, inflammatory processes, or hormonal changes, affect the evenness of skin tone and, in some cases, directly influence self-esteem. As diverse as their causes may be, the correct approach can significantly reduce their appearance, promoting a more even, luminous, and healthy complexion. Natural cosmetics offer gentle and effective alternatives, exploring the benefits of ingredients such as clay, vegetable oils, and antioxidants, which lighten and revitalize without harming the skin.

Prevention is the first step in caring for spots, with daily sun protection being one of the most important strategies. Exposure to UV rays, even on cloudy days, is the main cause of increased melanin production, the pigment that, when accumulated irregularly, gives rise to spots. In addition, habits such as avoiding the sun during peak hours and wearing hats and clothing that block ultraviolet radiation complement topical protection. At the same time, adopting a diet rich in antioxidants, such as vitamins C and E, strengthens the skin from the inside out, helping to fight free radicals that accelerate aging and promote hyperpigmentation.

Natural cosmetics present a comprehensive set of solutions to even out skin tone and minimize blemishes. Among the most common types, melasma stands out as a challenging condition. These dark spots, usually located in areas such as the forehead, cheeks, nose, and chin, are strongly linked to hormonal factors and sun exposure, in addition to genetic predisposition. Natural treatment can help to gradually soften them, protecting and regenerating the skin. Freckles, in turn, have a genetic origin, but their intensity increases with sun exposure, making daily use of sunscreen essential.

Age spots, which appear with aging, are caused by the accumulation of melanin over time in frequently exposed areas such as the face, hands, and arms. These spots respond well to gentle lightening ingredients, such as white clay. Acne spots and post-inflammatory hyperchromia, resulting from inflammatory processes, arise from excess melanin in the injured area and can be treated with antioxidant and regenerating ingredients.

The causes of spots are diverse, but excessive sun exposure is the main culprit. UV rays stimulate the production of melanin, essential for protecting the skin, but when in excess, they lead to the appearance of spots. Hormonal changes also play an important role, especially in conditions such as melasma, which is exacerbated during pregnancy or with the use of contraceptives. Other factors, such as aging and inflammation, aggravate the condition, while genetic predisposition determines the intensity and frequency of these changes.

Prevention is key to minimizing the appearance of spots. Using sunscreen daily, with a sun protection factor of 30 or higher, is essential. Reapplication every two hours, especially after swimming or sweating, enhances the effects. In addition, avoiding sun exposure between 10 am and 4 pm and wearing accessories such as hats and sunglasses help protect the skin. Diet also plays an important role: including foods rich in antioxidants, such as citrus fruits, leafy greens, and nuts, helps fight free radicals.

To treat existing spots, natural recipes offer accessible and effective solutions. The white clay lightening mask is a practical and powerful example. To prepare it, mix two tablespoons of white clay with one tablespoon of rose hydrosol and five drops of lavender essential oil, forming a creamy paste. Applied to clean skin, the mask acts for 15 to 20 minutes, helping to lighten and soften the skin.

Another option is the vitamin C lightening serum, prepared with one tablespoon of rosehip vegetable oil and half a teaspoon of vitamin C powder. Stored in a dark glass bottle, it should be applied at night, before bed. Vitamin C, with its antioxidant properties, reduces blemishes and promotes skin regeneration. Rosehip lightening oil can be used directly on the affected areas, being gently massaged at night, before bed, to stimulate cell regeneration.

When adopting these treatments, it is essential to perform a sensitivity test before use to avoid adverse reactions. As lightening products can increase the skin's sensitivity to the sun, they should be used at night and always accompanied by sun protection during the day. In addition, results may take weeks or months to become visible, requiring patience and consistency.

Integrating these natural practices into a care routine that includes sun protection, a healthy diet, and regular hydration provides more even and healthy skin. If blemishes persist or worsen, consultation with a dermatologist is recommended to investigate the causes and personalize treatment. Taking care of your skin is not just an aesthetic issue, but an act of well-being and self-acceptance that promotes confidence and lasting health.

Maintaining healthy, even skin is a reflection of ongoing care and conscious choices, where the combination of prevention, natural treatments, and lifestyle changes plays a crucial role. By incorporating solutions such as white clay masks, vitamin C serums, and regenerating oils, it is possible to promote results that not only smooth blemishes but also nourish and revitalize the skin as a whole. This harmonious approach rescues the essence of self-care, valuing each step of the process.

In addition to topical treatments, it is essential to remember that the state of the skin reflects the health of the body as a whole. A balanced diet, rich in antioxidants, combined with adequate water intake, strengthens the skin internally, complementing external care. These habits not only help prevent new blemishes but also create an environment conducive to cell regeneration, promoting long-lasting results and a luminous and vibrant appearance.

Caring for skin spots is not a temporary commitment, but a long-term investment in well-being and self-esteem. Adopting consistent and natural practices, aligned with individual needs, provides benefits that go beyond appearance. This journey, guided by patience and dedication, transforms the relationship with one's own skin, reaffirming the power of conscious and gentle choices that promote balance and confidence.

# Chapter 15
# Facial Rejuvenation

Skin aging reflects a natural process that, although inevitable, can be significantly delayed with consistent care and preventive strategies. As the years go by, internal and external changes shape the appearance of the skin, the most evident being the reduction of collagen and elastin, which compromises firmness and elasticity. In addition, factors such as sun exposure, pollution, stress, poor diet, and harmful habits, such as smoking, accelerate the signs of aging, resulting in wrinkles, expression lines, blemishes, and dryness. Despite this, an approach combining healthy habits and natural cosmetics allows you to preserve the vitality of your skin and promote a more youthful and balanced appearance.

Daily sun protection is one of the pillars of preventing premature aging. UV rays, when they reach the skin, stimulate the degradation of collagen and elastin, in addition to generating free radicals, unstable molecules that accelerate cell damage. Wearing adequate sunscreen, combined with physical barriers such as hats and protective clothing, significantly reduces these effects. At the same time, a routine that includes cleansing, toning, and moisturizing the skin keeps its protective barrier intact, promoting cell renewal and improving texture and natural radiance.

The benefits of natural cosmetics, which integrate antioxidants, vegetable oils, and regenerating ingredients, are a highlight in this care. Substances such as rosehip oil, known for its ability to stimulate cell regeneration, and vitamin C, a potent antioxidant, are particularly effective in minimizing fine lines, improving luminosity, and evening out skin tone. Natural masks and serums, prepared with elements such as aloe vera and white clay, offer deep hydration and combat dryness, promoting more vibrant and elastic skin. Thus, by combining this care with a balanced lifestyle and dermatological monitoring, it is possible to prolong the youthfulness of the skin and enjoy a healthy and radiant appearance.

Natural cosmetics present a delicate yet efficient approach to promoting facial rejuvenation, valuing ingredients with properties that not only treat but also prevent the signs of aging. Through antioxidant, moisturizing, regenerating, and nourishing elements, it is possible to obtain firmer, smoother, more luminous skin with a visibly rejuvenated appearance. This approach includes both understanding the causes of aging and applying specific and personalized care.

The skin aging process is intricate, combining intrinsic and extrinsic factors that affect its appearance and health over time. Intrinsic factors, such as genetics and chronological aging, play an inevitable role, determining the basic structure of the skin and its ability to produce collagen and elastin. Genetics, for example, is responsible for traits such as a predisposition to sagging or the early formation of expression lines, while the passing of years naturally reduces firmness and elasticity, resulting in wrinkles and changes in texture.

On the other hand, extrinsic factors, which include sun exposure, pollution, smoking, inadequate diet, stress, and sleep deprivation, are responsible for accelerating this natural process. Ultraviolet radiation is particularly harmful, causing deep cell damage and the degradation of collagen and elastin fibers, which leads to the formation of spots and wrinkles. Environmental pollution contributes by generating free radicals that damage the skin, while smoking decreases oxygenation and blood circulation, amplifying the signs of aging. A diet rich in sugar and processed foods, coupled with chronic stress and lack of sleep, also compromises cell renewal and skin health.

Preventing premature aging requires a multifaceted approach, starting with daily sun protection. The use of sunscreens with SPF 30 or higher, applied even on cloudy days and reapplied every two hours, is essential. In addition, avoiding sun exposure during peak hours, between 10 am and 4 pm, and adopting the use of hats, light clothing, and sunglasses helps to minimize the damage caused by UV rays. At the same time, a diet rich in fruits, vegetables, and greens, combined with adequate water intake, is essential to provide the nutrients necessary for skin regeneration and eliminate toxins.

Maintaining a basic care routine, such as cleansing and moisturizing with gentle products, completes the basis of this prevention. These practices, together with quitting smoking, controlling stress through techniques such as yoga or meditation, and good quality sleep, provide an environment conducive to cell regeneration and the preservation of youthful skin.

Among natural treatments, homemade recipes stand out for their simplicity and effectiveness. A rejuvenating facial serum made with rosehip oil and vitamin C, for example, is a powerful alternative to stimulate cell renewal and fight free radicals. Just mix one tablespoon of rosehip vegetable oil with half a teaspoon of vitamin C powder, storing the product in a dark glass bottle. Applied at night to clean skin, the serum helps to restore skin firmness and luminosity.

Another solution is the white clay and aloe vera face mask, which combines two tablespoons of clay with the same amount of aloe vera gel and one teaspoon of honey. This preparation forms a creamy paste, ideal for applying to clean skin, remaining for 15 to 20 minutes before being removed with warm water. The clay, with its purifying properties, combined with the hydration of aloe vera and honey, provides a feeling of freshness and revitalization.

Avocado and argan oil cream is especially indicated to deeply moisturize and restore elasticity. Prepared with a quarter of mashed ripe avocado, one tablespoon of argan oil, and one teaspoon of honey, it should be applied with gentle movements until fully absorbed, offering visible results with regular use.

These recipes can be enhanced by additional practices, such as facial massage and gymnastics for the facial muscles, which stimulate blood circulation and collagen production. Circular and upward movements, performed daily, not only tone the skin but also help relieve tension, while specific exercises delay sagging.

The continuous use of natural cosmetics, chosen according to individual needs, is also an effective way to prolong results. Ingredients such as rosehip, vitamin C, aloe vera, and white clay have proven regenerating and antioxidant properties, being powerful allies in maintaining skin health. However, it is essential to seek the guidance of a dermatologist, who will be able to assess the skin and suggest personalized strategies to optimize care.

Therefore, facial rejuvenation is not an isolated event, but a daily commitment to one's own health and well-being. By combining healthy habits, natural treatments, and professional support, it is possible not only to delay the signs of aging but also to cultivate radiant and vital skin, reflecting a beauty that transcends time.

Facial rejuvenation goes beyond just preserving a youthful appearance; it celebrates self-care, transforming daily routines into rituals that nourish the skin and spirit. By integrating natural solutions such as clay masks and antioxidant serums into a balanced lifestyle, a solid foundation for skin health is created. These simple but effective steps not only delay the signs of aging but also promote a renewed sense of confidence and well-being.

Consistency is the key element in this journey. Choosing products and practices that respect the individual needs of the skin, such as facial massages that activate circulation and natural recipes full of nutrients, reinforces the connection between external and internal care. In addition, habits such as sun protection, a diet rich in antioxidants, and regular hydration ensure that each effort is supported by healthy and lasting foundations.

The skin, over time, tells life stories, and taking care of it is a gesture of respect for these narratives. With patience, dedication, and conscious choices, it is possible to create a routine that not only combats the effects of time but also values individuality and the vitality that only experience can bring. This is the true purpose of rejuvenation: skin that not only reflects youth but also balance and joy.

# Chapter 16
# Natural Sun Protection

Exposure to sunlight is an essential part of human life, as it plays a fundamental role in vitamin D synthesis and contributes to the balance of physical and emotional well-being. However, direct and prolonged contact with the sun's rays without proper protection can trigger a series of damages to the skin, ranging from temporary burns to more serious consequences, such as premature aging and a significant increase in the risk of skin cancer. In this context, protecting the skin consciously, using effective and safe resources, becomes an indispensable priority to preserve both health and appearance over time.

Sunlight emits ultraviolet (UV) rays, classified as UVA and UVB, which directly impact the skin. While UVA rays penetrate deeper, causing aging and cumulative damage to collagen, UVB rays are primarily responsible for sunburn and cell mutations that can lead to cancer. Awareness of these effects is crucial to encourage the adoption of preventive measures, such as the use of physical and chemical barriers, in addition to a reassessment of the role of natural cosmetics. Natural ingredients with photoprotective properties emerge as promising alternatives to conventional products, offering benefits without compromising skin health or the environment.

Adopting preventive habits doesn't just mean applying sunscreen routinely, but also embracing a broader approach that includes choosing safe products, mechanical protection, such as clothing and accessories, and moderate sun exposure at safer times. The focus on natural solutions also promotes a reconnection with simple and effective ingredients, such as vegetable and mineral oils with UV reflecting properties, contributing to more conscious and sustainable care. The combination of these practices reinforces the commitment to healthy, protected and well-cared for skin, while valuing the harmony between human well-being and environmental responsibility.

Protecting your skin from the sun is a fundamental habit to maintain its health and beauty over time, especially in a world where excessive sun exposure has become a global concern. While conventional sunscreens play an essential role in protecting against ultraviolet (UV) rays, many formulas include chemicals that can cause irritation, trigger allergies, or even affect the environment. Natural cosmetics emerge as a sustainable and effective solution, offering safe alternatives that use natural ingredients with photoprotective properties.

The importance of sun protection transcends aesthetic care, being an essential element in the prevention of serious conditions, such as skin cancer. Daily use of sunscreen, even on cloudy or rainy days, significantly reduces the risk of this disease, which is one of the most common in the world. Furthermore, premature aging, often marked by wrinkles, sagging and blemishes, can also be avoided with the regular application of photoprotective products. Protecting the skin prevents UVB rays from causing painful sunburn, while UVA rays, which penetrate deeper, are blocked, preventing cumulative damage to collagen and elastin.

The harms of excessive sun exposure are wide-ranging and go beyond what can be observed superficially. Sunburns not only cause immediate redness and pain, but also increase the risk of genetic changes that can lead to skin cancer. Skin blemishes, such as melasma or age spots, often result from inadequate sun exposure, as does photosensitivity, which makes the skin more vulnerable to irritation. In addition, there is a potential suppression of the immune system with prolonged exposure, which compromises the body's natural defense against infections.

Natural cosmetics offer innovative and effective solutions to meet the growing demand for products that are safe for the consumer and the environment. Ingredients such as vegetable and mineral oils play crucial roles in protecting against damage caused by UV radiation. Coconut oil, for example, has a natural sun protection factor (SPF) that varies between 4 and 10, while raspberry seed oil has an impressive SPF, between 28 and 50, making it an excellent choice for topical applications. Likewise, carrot oil, with an SPF between 38 and 40, is highly effective when used in combination formulas.

Natural minerals, such as zinc oxide and titanium dioxide, are widely recognized for their photoprotective properties. Both form a physical barrier on the skin that reflects solar radiation, offering broad protection against UVA and UVB rays. However, it is essential to ensure that these ingredients are used in their non-nano forms, preventing their absorption by the skin and ensuring greater safety.

Homemade recipes for natural sunscreens are a practical and economical way to incorporate these substances into everyday life. A simple sunscreen can be prepared by combining two tablespoons of coconut oil, one tablespoon of shea butter, and two tablespoons of non-nano particulate zinc oxide. Shea butter should be melted in a bain-marie before being mixed with other ingredients. The final product can be stored in a clean, dry container, applied 30 minutes before sun exposure, and reapplied every two hours or after activities such as swimming or excessive sweating.

Another option is sunscreen made with raspberry seed oil, a high SPF ingredient that can be combined with a tablespoon of jojoba oil and a tablespoon of non-nano particulate zinc oxide. The mixture should be well homogenized and applied in a similar way, ensuring efficient and natural protection against the sun's rays.

Taking a conscious approach also includes complementary practices, such as wearing appropriate clothing to block UV radiation. Wide-brimmed hats, sunglasses with UV protection, and clothing made from light but dense fabrics help reduce direct exposure. In addition, avoiding the sun during peak hours, generally between 10 am and 4 pm, is an important strategy to minimize risks.

The effectiveness of any sun protection routine also depends on how the products are applied. Sunscreen should be used generously, covering all exposed areas, and reapplied frequently. Choosing the right SPF for each skin type and activity is essential to ensure that protection is sufficient. For those with very fair or sensitive skin, opting for a higher SPF is recommended, while darker skin tones can benefit from moderate levels of protection.

Furthermore, regularly observing the skin for changes is an essential habit for early detection of problems. Spots, moles or lesions that change in size, color or shape should be evaluated by a dermatologist, who can also provide personalized guidance on the best protection methods and specific care.

Natural sun protection is not just a health issue, but also a conscious choice that promotes a balance between personal care and environmental preservation. By incorporating natural ingredients, homemade recipes and responsible habits, it is possible not only to prevent damage caused by UV radiation, but also to foster a more sustainable and harmonious lifestyle. This care, when adopted consistently, guarantees not only healthy and beautiful skin, but also a positive impact on the environment and quality of life.

Skin care goes beyond immediate protection from the sun's rays. It reflects a commitment to one's own well-being and to the environment in which we live. By choosing natural solutions, we are not only minimizing the impact of chemical substances on the body and the ecosystem, but also embracing practices that value the simplicity and effectiveness of the resources that nature offers us. This movement also invites us to re-evaluate our habits, incorporating more conscious choices into our daily routine.

The search for natural alternatives is, at the same time, a way to protect the skin and to reconnect with the essence of human care: respecting our body and the environment. Oils, minerals and practices such as avoiding peak sun hours become powerful allies in building a healthier and more sustainable life. In addition, the use of appropriate clothing and accessories is not just physical protection, but an act of respect for one's own health, complementing the use of natural or commercial formulas.

This commitment to natural sun protection reflects a broader vision of self-care and responsibility. It reminds us that every decision has a lasting impact, not just on appearance, but also on quality of life and the world around us. By consciously adopting preventive measures, we cultivate not only healthy skin, but also a deeper connection with nature, integrating harmony and balance into every daily choice.

# Chapter 17
# Body Scrub

Just as it happens naturally with the face, the skin of the body is also subject to the constant accumulation of dead cells, pollution residues, toxins and impurities that interfere with its appearance and health. When neglected, these conditions result in dull-looking skin, rough texture and a feeling of discomfort. Body exfoliation, therefore, emerges as an indispensable practice to promote cell renewal, improve skin texture and restore its natural glow. This care goes beyond a simple beauty ritual; it is an important step for the overall health of the skin, offering benefits that are reflected in both appearance and well-being.

The body exfoliation process allows the most superficial layers of the skin to be gently renewed, eliminating barriers that hinder the penetration of cosmetic treatments and leaving the skin surface more receptive to hydration. In addition, the friction of the exfoliants stimulates local blood circulation, increasing oxygenation and cell nutrition, which contributes to a more vibrant and healthy appearance. For people who face problems such as ingrown hairs, blackheads or a tendency to form pimples, this habit can help prevent inflammation and clogged pores, providing more even and flawless skin.

Opting for natural scrubs adds an extra dimension of care, as these products are free of harsh chemicals that can cause adverse reactions, especially on sensitive skin. Ingredients such as sugar, sea salt, coffee and clays not only cleanse the skin, but also offer specific benefits, such as antioxidant and soothing properties. By integrating body exfoliation into your weekly routine, with the choice of a product that respects the specific needs of your skin, it is possible to achieve results that go beyond aesthetics, promoting lasting comfort, balance and vitality.

The practice of body exfoliation is much more than a simple beauty ritual; it is essential care for the health and vitality of the skin. Over time, the skin of the body accumulates dead cells, pollution residues and other impurities that can interfere with its appearance and functionality. When neglected, these factors result in a rough texture, a dull appearance and a feeling of discomfort. Exfoliation then emerges as an effective method to remove these barriers, stimulate cell renewal and reveal younger, more even and healthy skin.

The benefits of this care go beyond the physical aspect. Body exfoliation not only removes dead cells, but also unclogs pores and improves skin texture, making it more receptive to the active ingredients of moisturizers and other cosmetics. This process, in addition to helping to prevent problems such as blackheads, pimples and ingrown hairs, also promotes better blood circulation, which contributes to the oxygenation and nutrition of cells. As a result, the skin takes on a more vibrant, radiant and well-cared for appearance.

Choosing natural scrubs for this routine adds an extra layer of care, as these products are formulated without harsh chemical additives that can cause irritation, especially on sensitive skin. Ingredients such as sugar, sea salt, coffee and clays are examples of simple but highly effective components. Each of these elements offers unique properties, such as antioxidant, soothing or purifying action, making them versatile allies in the search for healthy and balanced skin.

The benefits of body exfoliation are wide-ranging and transformative. Cell renewal, for example, is one of the main objectives of this care. By removing the surface layer of dead cells, exfoliation stimulates the skin's natural regeneration, revealing a smoother, more even and youthful surface. Another important point is the removal of accumulated impurities, such as excessive oiliness and pollution residues, which can clog pores and trigger inflammation.

For those who suffer from ingrown hairs, exfoliation is an indispensable step. By releasing trapped hairs under the skin, it reduces inflammation and the chance of developing folliculitis. In addition, the texture of the skin is also visibly improved with the regular use of exfoliants, which leave the surface softer and smoother to the touch.

Preparing the skin for hydration is another notable benefit. Without the barrier of dead cells, moisturizers and cosmetic treatments can penetrate deeper, enhancing their effects. As a bonus, the massage performed during the application of exfoliants provides relaxation and well-being, transforming the care into a pleasurable and invigorating moment.

The types of scrubs available vary in composition and action, allowing customization of care according to the needs of each skin type. Scrubs with natural granules, such as sugar, sea salt and fruit seeds, use friction to remove dead skin cells. Chemical peels, which contain acids such as glycolic or salicylic and enzymes such as papain, promote peeling in a smoother and more uniform way.

Choosing the ideal scrub depends on the specific characteristics of your skin. For normal skin, almost all types of scrubs are suitable, as long as they are used in moderation. Those with dry skin should prioritize options with fine granules and moisturizing ingredients, such as sugar and oats. For oily skin, scrubs with coarser granules, such as sea salt and coffee, are ideal, as they help control excess oil. Sensitive skin benefits from gentle exfoliants, such as white clay and oats, avoiding harsher chemicals.

Homemade natural body scrub recipes are an accessible and effective way to incorporate this care into your routine. A simple sugar and coconut oil scrub, for example, combines a cup of granulated sugar with half a cup of coconut oil. This mixture should be applied to damp body, with gentle circular motions, and rinsed with warm water to reveal hydrated and renewed skin.

Another popular recipe is the sea salt and lavender essential oil scrub, made with a cup of fine salt, half a cup of sweet almond vegetable oil and ten drops of lavender essential oil. This combination not only exfoliates, but also relaxes the senses, providing complete care for body and mind.

The coffee and honey scrub, in turn, is ideal for those looking for antioxidant and energizing properties. Just mix a cup of used coffee grounds with half a cup of honey and a quarter cup of coconut oil. The application follows the same principle: gentle circular movements on the damp body, followed by rinsing with warm water.

To ensure the best results, some practical tips are essential. Start by preparing your skin with a warm bath to moisten it and open your pores. Apply the chosen scrub in circular motions, paying special attention to rougher areas such as elbows, knees and heels. After rinsing the product well, finish by applying a natural body moisturizer to nourish the skin and prolong the benefits of exfoliation.

The frequency of this care should be adjusted to individual needs. In general, exfoliating the body once or twice a week is enough to keep the skin healthy and well-cared for, avoiding dryness or irritation.

Incorporating body exfoliation into your routine is not just a gesture of personal care, but also an opportunity to reconnect with your own body and with natural ingredients that offer exceptional benefits. By adopting simple and effective practices, it is possible to transform the skin, revealing its natural beauty and promoting well-being that transcends the surface.

By adopting the practice of body exfoliation, we not only take care of the skin, but also create a moment of connection with ourselves, a moment dedicated to renewal and self-care. This ritual, which combines simple techniques with the use of natural ingredients, stimulates the feeling of comfort and balance, reinforcing the importance of small gestures that can transform our routine. The positive impact goes beyond the physical, as the softness of revitalized skin also reflects emotional well-being, promoted by the attention dedicated to this process.

The diversity of options for body exfoliation allows each person to find the most appropriate approach to their needs. Whether through homemade recipes or ready-made products, scrubs have the power to adapt to individual lifestyles and preferences, making the practice accessible and personalized. This care also encourages us to reflect on the sustainability of our choices, seeking alternatives that respect both the body and the environment.

Thus, body exfoliation is established as more than just a step in a beauty routine; it becomes a transformative habit that combines health, aesthetics and pleasure. With each new application, the skin is renewed and revitalized, while the individual rediscovers himself in a moment of pause and care. This simple but meaningful practice is a reminder that self-care is a form of self-love that benefits not only the body, but also the mind and spirit.

# Chapter 18
# Body Hydration

Body hydration is one of the most important pillars for maintaining the health and appearance of the skin, ensuring that it remains protected, supple, and with a pleasant texture. The skin plays a vital role as a protective barrier for the body, but its constant exposure to environmental factors, such as dry weather, pollution, and solar radiation, can compromise its functions and lead to the loss of water and essential nutrients. When properly hydrated, the skin presents greater resistance to these aggressions, in addition to a naturally healthy and radiant appearance.

Hydration replenishment helps to strengthen the skin's protective layer, restoring its elasticity and preventing discomfort such as dryness and itching. In addition, well-hydrated skin reflects light better, resulting in a natural glow that highlights its vitality. However, effective hydration is not limited to the application of topical products; it also requires attention to the consumption of water and nutrients that favor skin health from the inside out. Thus, the combination of internal and external care forms the basis for balanced skin that is resistant to adverse everyday conditions.

Choosing natural moisturizing products is a way to offer the skin the necessary support without exposing it to potentially harmful chemicals. Ingredients such as vegetable oils and natural butters are highly nutritious and have properties that go beyond hydration, helping in cell regeneration and protection against premature aging. Incorporating this care into your daily routine allows you to not only preserve the integrity of your skin, but also create moments of self-care that benefit both body and mind.

Body hydration is one of the most important fundamentals to ensure the health and beauty of the skin, allowing it to maintain its protective function and a radiant appearance. The skin, as the largest organ in the human body, plays a crucial role in defending against external agents, but it is constantly exposed to environmental factors that can compromise its integrity. Dry weather, pollution, solar radiation, and even everyday habits, such as hot baths and the use of harsh soaps, contribute to the loss of water and essential nutrients. When properly hydrated, the skin not only resists these challenges better, but also exhibits natural elasticity, softness, and luminosity.

Effective hydration goes beyond the simple act of applying creams and oils to the skin. It involves integrated care, which combines adequate intake of fluids and nutrients with the choice of products that complement individual needs. Well-hydrated skin reflects more light, standing out for its vitality and softness. In addition, proper hydration restores elasticity, prevents discomfort such as dryness and itching, and protects against premature aging, contributing to a youthful and healthy appearance.

Among the many factors that affect skin hydration, the use of natural cosmetics is a choice that benefits both health and the environment. Ingredients such as vegetable oils, natural butters, and botanical extracts are rich in nutrients, vitamins, and antioxidants, offering deep hydration and protection against external aggressions. By opting for these elements, the risks associated with chemical compounds that can cause irritation or allergies are avoided, especially in more sensitive skin.

The importance of body hydration goes beyond its aesthetic dimension. Hydrated skin maintains the integrity of the skin barrier, which is essential for protection against microorganisms, pollution, and solar radiation. In addition, hydration prevents dryness, which can lead to roughness, flaking, and discomfort. Skin elasticity is also favored, making it more resistant to the appearance of stretch marks and sagging. As an added benefit, hydration helps in cell renewal, contributing to rejuvenated skin with a uniform texture.

However, factors such as long, hot baths, harsh soaps, excessive sun exposure, dry weather, and prolonged use of air conditioning are great enemies of hydration. With aging, the skin's natural oil production decreases, further aggravating dryness. To mitigate these effects, it is essential to adopt healthy habits, such as avoiding hot baths, using mild soaps, and maintaining a diet rich in nutrients and antioxidants.

Natural body moisturizers offer an effective and nourishing solution to restore and preserve skin hydration. Vegetable oils such as coconut, sweet almond, argan, and rosehip are rich in fatty acids and vitamins, providing deep hydration and cell regeneration. Natural butters, such as shea, cocoa, and cupuaçu, have a creamy texture and offer intense hydration, being especially indicated for dry or dehydrated skin. Aloe vera, in turn, combines moisturizing, soothing, and healing properties, making it an excellent choice for sensitive or irritated skin. Hydrolates, such as rose water and lavender, also have toning and soothing properties, making them ideal for light hydration.

Homemade natural moisturizer recipes are simple and effective. A lotion made with aloe vera gel and coconut oil, for example, combines intense hydration with soothing properties. Just mix half a cup of aloe vera gel with a quarter cup of coconut oil until it forms a homogeneous lotion, which can be applied to damp skin after bathing, ensuring rapid absorption and long-lasting softness.

Another recipe is the shea butter and sweet almond oil moisturizing cream. To prepare it, melt half a cup of shea butter in a bain-marie and add a quarter cup of sweet almond oil. For a relaxing touch, you can add ten drops of lavender essential oil. This cream is ideal for deeply nourishing dry skin, leaving it soft and renewed.

To optimize the benefits of body hydration, some practices are essential. Drinking at least two liters of water a day is essential to keep your skin hydrated from the inside out. Short, warm baths help preserve the skin's natural oils, as does the use of neutral or slightly acidic soaps. Moisturizers should be applied immediately after bathing, while the skin is still damp, to maximize absorption and seal in moisture. In addition, exfoliating the skin weekly removes dead cells and improves the penetration of moisturizing products.

Wearing comfortable clothes made of cotton allows the skin to breathe and prevents the accumulation of sweat, which can aggravate dryness. Protecting the skin from the sun with daily sunscreen is another essential measure to prevent dehydration caused by UV radiation.

Body hydration is, therefore, an indispensable care to keep the skin young, lush, and healthy. Incorporating these habits into your daily routine, using natural products and prioritizing a holistic approach, provides not only benefits for the skin, but also an opportunity for self-care and connection with your own body. In this way, it is possible to cultivate soft, radiant skin that is resistant to everyday adversities, reflecting balance and well-being.

The practice of body hydration not only preserves skin health, but also elevates the self-care experience to a deeper level. By dedicating moments to apply lotions or oils with attention and delicacy, a space for pause is created amidst the demands of everyday life, strengthening the relationship between body and mind. This simple ritual invites us to value touch and presence, making daily care an opportunity to renew energies and cultivate integral well-being.

In addition to the immediate benefits, hydration promotes a virtuous cycle that has a long-term impact. Properly nourished skin better copes with climate variations and natural aging, remaining resistant and with a luminous appearance. This regular care strengthens the skin's protective barrier, allowing it to fulfill its essential function of protecting the body against external aggressions, while remaining soft and comfortable to the touch.

By integrating body hydration into your routine, whether through natural products or homemade techniques, we open space for a more conscious and harmonious lifestyle. This daily habit, although simple, is capable of transforming the relationship with one's own skin, reflecting not only in its appearance, but also in a lasting feeling of balance and serenity. In this way, taking care of the body becomes an act of self-love, bringing out the glow that comes from within.

# Chapter 19
# Cellulite: Natural Treatment

Cellulite is a widely known aesthetic condition that results from the interaction between internal and external factors that affect the structure of the skin and subcutaneous tissue. Characterized by ripples and depressions in the skin, it arises due to the irregular accumulation of fat, fluids, and toxins in the deeper layers of the skin, which compromises the uniform appearance. Although it is more prevalent in women, due to differences in the anatomy of connective tissue and the effects of female hormones, cellulite can also manifest itself in men, especially in cases related to weight gain or hormonal imbalances.

Understanding the underlying causes of cellulite is essential to seeking effective and sustainable solutions. Hormonal factors, especially high levels of estrogen, play a significant role by influencing fluid retention, blood circulation, and fat storage. In addition, genetic issues, inadequate eating habits, a sedentary lifestyle, and even stress can intensify the manifestation of cellulite over time. This condition is not just the result of a single element, but rather a complex interaction between natural predispositions and lifestyle choices.

The adoption of natural methods to combat cellulite has proven to be a promising and holistic approach, aligned with the search for healthier and more sustainable alternatives. By prioritizing ingredients with draining, antioxidant, and firming properties, such as caffeine, centella asiatica, and essential oils, it is possible to stimulate circulation, reduce fluid retention, and strengthen connective tissue. When combined with a routine of physical exercise, a balanced diet, and techniques such as lymphatic drainage, these natural treatments not only help to minimize cellulite, but also promote improvements in the overall health of the skin, resulting in a firmer, more uniform, and revitalized appearance.

Cellulite, a widely known aesthetic condition, reflects a complex interaction between internal and external factors that affect the structure of the skin and subcutaneous tissue. Although it does not represent a serious health problem, it can impact the self-esteem and well-being of many people. Characterized by ripples and depressions in the skin, cellulite results from a combination of fluid retention, accumulation of fat and toxins in the deeper layers of the skin. These factors, added to changes in the structure of connective tissue, compromise the uniform appearance of the skin.

Although more common in women, due to hormonal and anatomical differences, cellulite can also occur in men, mainly in cases associated with weight gain or hormonal imbalances. The natural approach to treating this condition not only helps to minimize its visual impact, but also promotes improvements in the overall health of the skin and body.

Understanding the causes of cellulite is a fundamental step in dealing with it effectively. Hormonal factors play a significant role in this process, especially high levels of estrogen, which can intensify fluid retention, compromise blood circulation, and stimulate fat accumulation. In addition, genetic factors influence individual predisposition, affecting skin structure and fat distribution. Poor circulation, inadequate eating habits, a sedentary lifestyle, smoking, and even stress contribute to the worsening of this condition.

The severity of cellulite varies in degrees. In grade 1, it is visible only when compressing or contracting the skin. In grade 2, the ripples are already perceptible to the naked eye. In grade 3, the irregularities become more pronounced, with deeper depressions, and in grade 4, there are severe ripples, often accompanied by pain and sensitivity to the touch. Identifying the degree of cellulite is essential to direct the most appropriate treatment strategies.

The natural approach to the treatment of cellulite has proven to be promising, providing sustainable and holistic solutions. The use of natural cosmetics with draining, firming, and circulation-activating properties is an effective strategy. Ingredients such as caffeine, centella asiatica, rosemary essential oil, and orange essential oil have proven properties that help fight cellulite. In addition, consuming a balanced diet, rich in fruits, vegetables, whole grains, and lean protein, also plays a crucial role in reducing cellulite, while processed foods high in sodium, sugar, and fat should be avoided.

Regular physical exercise is another essential component. Activities such as walking, running, swimming, and weight training help improve blood circulation, burn calories, and strengthen muscles, reducing the accumulation of subcutaneous fat. Adequate hydration, in turn, is essential to eliminate toxins and prevent fluid retention, while techniques such as lymphatic drainage and modeling massage complement the treatment, stimulating circulation and promoting the elimination of fluids and toxins.

Among the natural recipes to treat cellulite, the anti-cellulite cream with caffeine and centella asiatica stands out. To prepare it, simply melt half a cup of shea butter in a bain-marie, add a quarter cup of coconut oil, a tablespoon of centella asiatica extract, and two teaspoons of anhydrous caffeine. The mixture should be stored in a clean container and applied to the affected areas twice a day, with massages in circular motions.

Another effective option is the anti-cellulite massage oil with rosemary and orange. This oil combines half a cup of sweet almond oil with 10 drops of rosemary essential oil and 10 drops of sweet orange essential oil. After mixing the ingredients well, the oil should be stored in a dark bottle and used for daily massages in areas with cellulite.

The anti-cellulite body mask with green clay and ginger is also an excellent alternative. Mix two tablespoons of green clay with a tablespoon of grated ginger and filtered water until it forms a creamy paste.

Apply the mask to the affected areas, leave it on for 20 minutes and rinse with warm water. This combination promotes detoxification and improves skin texture.

To maximize results, some additional practices should be incorporated. Controlling stress, avoiding smoking, and maintaining patience and persistence are essential. Treating cellulite takes time and dedication, but adopting a holistic approach that includes internal and external care can transform the appearance of the skin and improve self-esteem.

Thus, combating cellulite naturally is more than an act of self-care; it is a commitment to overall well-being. By combining healthy habits with natural products and effective practices, it is possible to achieve more uniform, firm, and revitalized skin, reflecting health, balance, and confidence.

Treating cellulite naturally is a journey that goes beyond aesthetics, as it encompasses a transformation in lifestyle and the relationship with one's own body. Dedication to healthy practices, such as a balanced diet, regular physical exercise, and hydration, not only reduces the signs of cellulite, but also promotes lasting and integral well-being. This daily care reinforces the connection between internal health and external appearance, strengthening self-esteem and confidence.

The use of home treatments and natural cosmetics, combined with techniques such as massage and lymphatic drainage, enhances the results, offering accessible and effective alternatives. These practices value the power of natural ingredients and simplicity, demonstrating that body care can be sustainable and gentle. In addition, these moments of self-care provide relaxation and stress relief, reinforcing the importance of taking care not only of the skin, but also of emotional balance.

By integrating these natural strategies into your routine, it is possible to perceive significant changes in the texture and firmness of the skin. Persistence and commitment to this process reflect dedication to a holistic and conscious approach to health and beauty. More than a treatment, this practice becomes an act of affection and respect for oneself, revealing revitalized skin that reflects the strength and care that come from within.

# Chapter 20
# Stretch Marks: Prevention and Treatment

Stretch marks are marks that reflect the skin's adaptation process to sudden or significant changes in its structure, resulting from the rupture of collagen and elastin fibers, which guarantee its elasticity. When subjected to excessive or rapid stretching, such as those that occur during periods of accelerated growth, pregnancy, or weight gain, the skin may not be able to keep up with these transformations, generating the characteristic lines that initially appear reddish or purplish and, over time, become lighter. Although they do not pose direct health risks, stretch marks can cause aesthetic discomfort and emotional impact, and it is common to seek solutions that minimize their appearance.

The prevention of stretch marks is essential care that begins with maintaining skin health. This includes continuous hydration, both through adequate water consumption and the application of topical products rich in nourishing and regenerating ingredients, such as vegetable oils and natural butters. These elements help preserve the skin's elasticity and protect it against the impacts of bodily changes. Furthermore, a balanced diet rich in vitamins, minerals, and antioxidants also contributes to strengthening the skin's structure, reducing the risk of fiber rupture.

When stretch marks are already present, the natural approach offers solutions that aim to improve their appearance by stimulating skin regeneration. Ingredients such as rosehip oil, shea butter, and aloe vera have restorative and moisturizing properties that help smooth the texture and even out skin tone. Combined with regular massages, which activate blood circulation and promote the absorption of products, these treatments can significantly reduce the visibility of stretch marks. This combination of preventive and restorative care reinforces the importance of a dedicated and conscious routine to achieve healthier, more even, and resilient skin.

Stretch marks are marks that symbolize the skin's ability to adapt to abrupt changes in its structure. These lines, which can vary from reddish and purplish tones at the beginning to whitish over time, result from the rupture of collagen and elastin fibers, responsible for the skin's elasticity and firmness. Often associated with periods of rapid growth, such as puberty, pregnancy, or sudden weight gain, stretch marks do not pose health risks but can cause aesthetic and emotional discomfort, motivating the search for preventive and restorative solutions.

Preventing stretch marks is the most effective approach to minimizing their occurrence and involves constant care with skin health. Hydration is the first essential step, both through adequate water consumption and the application of products rich in vegetable oils and natural butters, such as coconut oil, rosehip oil, and shea butter. These ingredients promote deep nourishment and elasticity, helping the skin to better cope with stretching. In addition, a balanced diet rich in vitamins C and E, zinc, and antioxidants strengthens the skin's structure and contributes to its natural regeneration.

Stretch marks are largely formed due to the stretching of the skin beyond its ability to adapt. In adolescence, for example, accelerated growth can generate these marks in regions such as the thighs, hips, and breasts. During pregnancy, the abdomen, hips, and breasts are particularly prone areas due to rapid volume gain. Hormonal changes, such as those that occur during puberty, menopause, or even due to medications such as corticosteroids, also play an important role, affecting the skin's elasticity and increasing its susceptibility to rupture.

Genetic predisposition is another factor that directly influences the risk of developing stretch marks. People with a family history are more likely to have them, as are women, due to hormonal and structural differences in the skin. Furthermore, hormonal changes associated with pregnancy or the use of specific medications can aggravate the problem. Age also plays a role, with adolescence and pregnancy being the most critical periods for the appearance of these marks.

When stretch marks are already present, natural treatment emerges as an effective alternative to soften their appearance. Vegetable oils such as rosehip, rich in vitamin C and fatty acids, have regenerating properties that help even out skin tone and reduce the visibility of marks. Coconut oil and shea butter, in turn, offer deep hydration and promote elasticity, essential for the recovery of the affected tissue. Aloe vera combines soothing and healing properties, aiding in regeneration and reducing inflammation.

Regular massage in the affected areas is a key element in the treatment of stretch marks. By activating blood circulation and improving the absorption of products, it enhances the effects of the applied ingredients and stimulates the production of collagen, essential for skin regeneration. This practice, combined with the consistent use of natural products, can generate significant improvements in the texture and appearance of the skin.

Homemade recipes offer accessible and effective options for dealing with stretch marks. A natural oil for stretch marks, made with 30 ml of rosehip oil, 10 ml of sweet almond oil, and the contents of a vitamin E capsule, is one example. Just mix the ingredients and apply them to the affected areas, massaging gently twice a day. This oil combines regenerating, antioxidant, and moisturizing properties, promoting cell renewal and skin tone uniformity.

Another alternative is shea butter and aloe vera stretch mark cream. Melt a quarter cup of shea butter in a bain-marie and mix with a quarter cup of aloe vera gel and, optionally, 10 drops of lavender essential oil. After mixing well, apply the cream to stretch marks with gentle massages, twice a day. This formula combines intense hydration and soothing properties, aiding in skin recovery.

The prevention and treatment of stretch marks require consistency and patience. In addition to keeping the skin hydrated daily with products rich in nutrients, it is important to adopt healthy habits, such as regular physical exercise and a balanced diet. Weight control, avoiding sudden variations, is also essential to reduce skin stretching and prevent new marks.

However, it is important to recognize that the stretch mark treatment process does not bring immediate results. Skin regeneration is gradual, and continuous care is essential to achieve visible improvement. Consulting a dermatologist in more severe or extensive cases may be necessary, ensuring the choice of the most appropriate approaches for each situation.

By adopting a dedicated routine that includes prevention and treatment with natural products and healthy habits, it is possible to significantly minimize the appearance of stretch marks and promote more even and resilient skin. This care also contributes to strengthening self-esteem and a more positive relationship with one's own body, reflecting health and confidence in every detail.

Stretch marks, although natural and common, carry stories of changes and adaptations in the body and are often seen as marks of transformation. Prevention and care are essential allies to maintain healthy skin and minimize these marks, but it is also important to recognize that each line is part of each person's individuality. Adopting a balanced and kind approach to one's own body is as fundamental as the treatments that aim to improve its appearance.

The use of natural treatments, combined with patience and consistency, can bring significant results in the texture and uniformity of the skin. Each massage with regenerating oils, each application of a nourishing cream, is a gesture of self-care that reinforces the positive relationship with one's own body. The combination of powerful ingredients from nature and healthy habits creates a solid foundation for resilient skin, with renewed elasticity and a revitalized appearance.

Taking care of stretch marks is more than just seeking aesthetic results; it is also an opportunity to strengthen self-esteem and celebrate the changes that shape who we are. Whether preventing new marks or treating existing ones, this process symbolizes a journey of caring for the body and oneself. By combining practice and acceptance, it is possible to achieve not only healthier skin but also a more harmonious and confident relationship with one's own image.

# Chapter 21
# Therapeutic Baths

Therapeutic baths are revealed as profoundly transformative practices that combine ancestral wisdom with the restorative potential of water and natural elements. Far from being mere routine actions, these baths constitute sacred moments of self-care and renewal, in which body and mind meet in perfect harmony. Combining herbs, flowers, and essential oils, each immersion becomes a unique sensory experience, capable of providing benefits that transcend the physical and reach the emotional and spiritual. They act as portals of healing, bringing energy balance, well-being, and an invitation to self-knowledge.

Water, the fundamental element of life, acquires an even deeper symbolic and therapeutic meaning when enriched with the properties of plants. Each natural ingredient contributes specific qualities that, when combined with the heat and flow of the liquid, intensify its power of healing and regeneration. Whether to relieve muscle aches, promote skin hydration, or restore mental vigor, therapeutic baths offer holistic solutions to the demands of a modern life full of stress and challenges. Thus, they become indispensable allies for those seeking an integrated approach to health and well-being.

By incorporating therapeutic baths into your routine, you are not only taking care of your body but also dedicating precious time to nourish your soul. Through the enveloping aroma of essential oils, the soft touch of petals, and the embracing water, a space of deep inner connection is created. This act of presence and attention to oneself allows each immersion to be more than just a relaxation ritual: it transforms into a path of reconnection and revitalization, essential to face daily challenges with balance, energy, and serenity.

Much more than simple hygiene, therapeutic baths offer an invitation to deep self-care, providing a moment of intimate connection with oneself. They allow the body to find relief from accumulated tension while the mind is enveloped in an atmosphere of calm and serenity. Each immersion is an opportunity to align body, mind, and spirit, benefiting from the therapeutic properties of plants in synergy with the regenerative power of water.

The benefits that therapeutic baths provide go far beyond simple relaxation. Warm water acts as a natural means of relieving stress, allowing muscles to loosen and the worries of everyday life to disappear, even if temporarily. Herbs and essential oils amplify this experience, creating a sense of well-being that lingers after the bath. Imagine the water enveloping the body while the subtle and comforting aromas of lavender or chamomile soothe the senses and promote a rare tranquility in hectic days.

Another aspect that deserves to be highlighted is the positive impact of therapeutic baths on blood circulation. The water temperature and the stimulating effects of ingredients such as rosemary help to dilate blood vessels, promoting more efficient circulation and oxygenation of tissues. This results in a feeling of revitalization that energizes the body and mind, preparing it for the challenges of everyday life.

Furthermore, muscle and joint pain finds relief in the analgesic and anti-inflammatory properties of specific herbs. Ingredients such as eucalyptus and calendula help reduce physical discomfort while promoting relaxation and general well-being. For those seeking relief from physical tension, these baths are a natural and effective solution.

The purification and detoxification of the body are also widely favored by therapeutic baths. The combination of sea salts or Himalayan salts with essential oils can help eliminate toxins through sweating, while the water deeply hydrates the skin, leaving it soft, revitalized, and radiant.

No less important, therapeutic baths also play an essential role in the body's energy balance. Ingredients such as roses and lemongrass help harmonize the chakras, creating a space of integral well-being that transcends the physical and reaches the emotional and spiritual. The practice of aromatherapy, present in the use of essential oils, complements this balance by bringing emotional benefits through aromas that stimulate feelings of comfort, energy, or tranquility.

The preparation of therapeutic baths is a ritual in itself, which can be customized according to needs and preferences. The infusion of herbs, for example, is a simple and effective technique: just put the herbs or flowers in boiling water, cover the container and let it rest for 15 to 20 minutes before straining and adding to the bath water. Decoction is indicated for more resistant ingredients, such as roots or bark, which need to be boiled for 10 to 15 minutes to release their properties. Both techniques capture the best of natural ingredients, ensuring the bath is rich in benefits.

Bath salts are another popular and versatile option. By mixing sea salt or Himalayan pink salt with dried herbs and essential oils, a powerful combination is created that purifies, relaxes, and detoxifies the body. Finally, the simplicity of essential oils should not be underestimated: a few drops directly into the bath water transform the moment into a complete sensory experience.

Each natural ingredient has its unique contribution. Lavender, for example, is known for its relaxing properties and for helping to combat stress and insomnia. Chamomile, in addition to being calming, is an excellent anti-inflammatory that also relieves skin irritations. Rosemary, on the other hand, stimulates circulation and revitalizes the body, while eucalyptus is ideal for decongesting the airways, being an ally in times of flu or colds. Roses promote self-love and self-esteem, making each bath a moment of self-worth.

Recipes for therapeutic baths are varied and can be adapted. A relaxing lavender bath, for example, requires only dried lavender flowers and boiling water to create an infusion that, added to the bath water, offers 20 to 30 minutes of pure relaxation. The energizing rosemary bath uses fresh leaves and a decoction to stimulate the senses and invigorate the body. For deep detoxification, the mixture of sea salt with eucalyptus essential oil creates a renewing experience that combines purification and muscle relaxation.

To maximize the benefits, preparing the environment is essential. The soft light of candles, relaxing music, and the delicate aroma of incense transform the space into a haven of peace. The water temperature should be pleasant, welcoming, without extremes, while staying in the bath for 20 to 30 minutes ensures the absorption of all therapeutic benefits. After bathing, it is important to moisturize the skin with vegetable oil or natural cream, preserving the softness and care provided by the practice.

The frequency of therapeutic baths can vary according to individual needs, but including this habit at least once a week is enough to keep the body and mind in balance. For moments of greater tension, an immersion can be the necessary gesture to restore serenity.

Therapeutic baths are, therefore, not just a self-care ritual but a true practice of integral well-being. Incorporating them into the routine is creating a special moment of connection with oneself, relieving stress, promoting harmony, and revitalizing the being on all levels.

The practice of therapeutic baths transcends the idea of a simple technique, transforming itself into an act of celebrating one's own being. By immersing ourselves in waters enriched with natural ingredients, we allow the healing properties of these elements to envelop us, bringing a profound balance that reverberates in all aspects of life. It is at this moment that time seems to slow down, and the simple act of taking care of oneself becomes a manifestation of love and respect for one's own existence.

The regenerative power of these baths is directly linked to the intention with which they are performed. Every detail - from the choice of herbs to the care with the atmosphere of the environment - contributes to a unique experience. More than relieving tension or invigorating the body, it is an opportunity to reconnect with our essence, a moment in which we allow ourselves to listen to the needs of our body and heart amidst the noise of everyday life. This return to the natural state of balance reminds us that true healing starts from the inside out.

At the end of each immersion, it is as if the water not only washes away impurities and tiredness but also returns us more whole, lighter, and prepared to face life with new eyes. Thus, therapeutic baths are not mere rituals; they are portals of transformation, where care for the body and spirit intertwine, leaving marks that echo far beyond the moment.

# Chapter 22
# Body Detoxification

Body detoxification emerges as an essential process to restore the body's harmony in a world increasingly saturated by toxins. Constantly exposed to pollution, processed foods, and daily stressors, the human body accumulates harmful substances that compromise its vital functions. This accumulation can cause fatigue, skin problems, digestive difficulties, and a series of other symptoms that reflect an internal imbalance. Promoting detoxification is, therefore, a natural and powerful way to revitalize the body, increase energy, and strengthen immunity, resulting in a healthier body and a clearer mind.

This process goes beyond specific measures, involving significant lifestyle changes. By prioritizing a nutrient-rich diet, hydrating properly, and integrating practices such as physical exercise and meditation, it is possible to enhance the body's natural ability to eliminate impurities. In addition, specific methods, such as detox juices, teas, and saunas, directly stimulate the excretory systems, aiding the liver, kidneys, and intestines in their functions. Each step taken on this detoxification path is also an act of self-care, promoting not only physical health but also emotional well-being.

Adopting a regular detoxification routine is an opportunity to reconnect with your own body, allowing it to function at its ideal state. This preventive care helps balance energy levels, improve sleep quality, and strengthen the immune system, protecting against disease. More than that, it is reflected externally, with more luminous and vibrant skin, and internally, with greater mental clarity and willingness. By incorporating these practices in a conscious and personalized way, you not only purify your body but also create a solid foundation for living a healthier and fuller life.

Body detoxification is a profound process that aims to help the body eliminate accumulated toxins, promoting an internal cleansing capable of restoring vitality and balance. By adopting healthy habits and using natural resources, it is possible to stimulate the excretory systems, improving blood and lymphatic circulation, in addition to favoring the elimination of impurities. This practice results not only in healthier, more radiant skin, but also in increased energy levels, improved sleep quality, and strengthened immunity.

One of the most visible benefits of detoxification is improved skin health. When accumulated toxins are eliminated, the skin gains a natural glow, reducing problems such as acne, dermatitis, and signs of premature aging. Furthermore, vital energy increases significantly, combating the feeling of persistent tiredness that often hinders productivity and well-being. At the same time, digestion is also benefited: by regulating the intestines and optimizing the absorption of nutrients, the body becomes more efficient and less prone to discomfort such as bloating and gas.

Another crucial aspect of detoxification is the strengthening of the immune system. A body free of toxins works more effectively in defending against disease, while the restful sleep that results from this practice further reinforces this protection. Furthermore, the elimination of retained fluids and the balance of the body can help in the weight loss process, in addition to reducing the appearance of cellulite and promoting a healthier body contour.

The benefits are not limited to the physical; detoxification also reflects on mental well-being. Mood is elevated, anxiety and stress decrease, and the mind finds greater clarity and balance. This process, by purifying the body, transforms into a journey of total renewal, touching both the exterior and the interior.

Identifying the signs that the body needs detoxification is essential to reap these benefits. Symptoms such as constant fatigue, skin problems, frequent headaches, digestive difficulties, and mood swings may indicate a buildup of toxins. Other signs include insomnia, fluid retention, low immunity, and even bad breath, often associated with an overloaded liver. Paying attention to these signs allows interventions to be made at the right time, preventing more serious problems.

Natural methods for detoxifying the body are varied and accessible. Diet plays a central role, with a focus on fruits, vegetables, whole grains, and lean proteins, while processed foods, sugars, and fats should be avoided. Detox juices, prepared with fresh ingredients such as kale, apple, and ginger, are a practical way to enrich the diet with vitamins, minerals, and antioxidants. Regular consumption of teas with detoxifying properties, such as green tea and hibiscus tea, also helps in the internal cleansing process.

Proper hydration is equally essential. Drinking at least two liters of water a day keeps the body functioning at its best, facilitating the elimination of toxins. The practice of physical exercise complements this effort, stimulating circulation and allowing sweat to play its role as a natural purification mechanism.

Complementary methods, such as saunas, foot baths, and lymphatic drainage, intensify the detoxification process. The sauna, for example, promotes sweating, while foot baths relax muscles, improve circulation, and contribute to the elimination of impurities. Lymphatic drainage, in turn, helps the lymphatic system play its role in eliminating toxins and fluids.

Furthermore, practices such as yoga and meditation offer mental and physical benefits. They help reduce stress, balance the body, and promote an overall state of well-being. The integration of these techniques creates a virtuous cycle, where body and mind work together to achieve balance and harmony.

Natural detoxification recipes are an effective way to incorporate these methods into everyday life. A green detox juice, for example, combines kale, green apple, cucumber, ginger, lemon juice, and coconut water to create a revitalizing drink. The detoxifying hibiscus tea, prepared with dried flowers and boiling water, is ideal to be consumed twice a day, hot or cold. For those seeking additional relaxation, a foot bath made with sea salt, apple cider vinegar, and lavender essential oil provides immediate relief while helping to eliminate toxins.

For effective body detoxification, it is important to follow some simple guidelines. Starting gradually allows the body to adapt to the process, while listening to the body's signals helps to adjust the intensity of the practices. Maintaining a regular detoxification routine is essential to achieve consistent results, and monitoring by a healthcare professional ensures that the process is safe and appropriate for individual needs.

By adopting body detoxification as part of your routine, you invest in long-term health. This care transforms not only the way you feel but also how you present yourself to the world, with more energy, willingness, and confidence. Incorporating healthy habits and using nature's resources is a path to a more balanced, fulfilling, and vitality-filled life.

Body detoxification is not just a health practice, but an invitation to a new relationship with your own body, based on care, attention, and balance. When starting this journey, we realize that it is not limited to eliminating toxins; it is a transformation that is reflected in greater willingness, mental clarity, and emotional lightness. Each action, from the conscious choice of food to the moments dedicated to meditation or relaxation, strengthens the connection with our integral well-being, promoting changes that transcend the physical.

The impact of this practice extends to all aspects of life, creating a solid foundation for habits that sustain a healthy routine. The body that renews itself through detoxification also becomes more resilient, facing daily challenges with renewed energy and a strengthened immunity. Small rituals, such as preparing a detox juice or enjoying a relaxing foot bath, become significant moments of self-care, rescuing the pleasure of taking care of yourself and providing balance in the midst of the daily rush.

This process, conducted with awareness and consistency, reveals that true detoxification goes beyond the physical, reaching the mind and spirit. By cleansing our interior, we open space for the new: new habits, new perspectives, and a new energy that drives us to live more fully. Thus, body detoxification becomes more than a purification method - it is a reunion with the best of ourselves, creating a path of vitality, harmony, and lasting well-being.

# Chapter 23
# Natural Hair Washing

Natural hair washing represents a careful and conscious approach that combines the effectiveness of natural ingredients with respect for the health of the hair and the environment. While conventional practices often expose hair to harsh chemicals that can cause long-term damage, the natural alternative emerges as a gentle and sustainable solution, ideal for those seeking to preserve the vitality and beauty of their hair. This form of care goes beyond hygiene: it is a true ritual of connection with nature and with one's own health.

Natural washing methods prioritize the elimination of impurities without compromising the integrity of the scalp and hair fiber. Ingredients such as saponified vegetable oils, clays, and plant extracts are carefully selected to offer balanced cleansing without removing the natural oils essential for protecting and nourishing the hair. In addition, options such as the use of solid shampoos and the No Poo method are ideal for reducing environmental impact, while providing effective results adaptable to different hair types.

Adopting natural hair washing is also a way to personalize hair care, choosing ingredients and methods that meet the specific needs of each hair type. Whether to moisturize dry hair, control oiliness, or preserve the definition of curls, natural resources offer a wide variety of versatile and beneficial options. By integrating these practices into your routine, you will be investing in hair care that unites well-being, sustainability, and respect for the essence of your hair, promoting healthy and conscious beauty.

Natural cosmetics provide a gentle and effective approach to hair washing, using natural ingredients that gently cleanse the hair and scalp without compromising hair health or the environment. This practice is an increasingly popular alternative among those who wish to take care of their hair in a conscious way, combining sustainability and effectiveness.

Natural washing methods, such as solid shampoos, natural liquid shampoos, No Poo, and Co-Wash, meet different hair needs. Solid shampoos, formulated with saponified vegetable oils, clays, and essential oils, are a practical and sustainable option. In bar format, they offer efficient cleaning without drying, while reducing the use of plastic packaging, minimizing environmental impact.

Natural liquid shampoos combine plant extracts, oils, and biodegradable surfactants, promoting gentle and versatile cleansing. For those seeking more specific methods, No Poo, which eliminates the use of shampoo, is ideal for curly, coily, and dry hair. Using only water, apple cider vinegar, or baking soda, this method preserves the hair's natural oils, helping to reduce frizz and dryness. Co-Wash, or conditioner washing, is an excellent choice for damaged or chemically treated hair, cleansing without damaging the strands.

Natural ingredients play a central role in these methods. Saponified vegetable oils, such as coconut, olive, palm, and castor oils, ensure balanced cleansing. Clays, such as white, green, and black, help purify and treat the scalp, while plant extracts, such as aloe vera, chamomile, and jaborandi, offer moisturizing and soothing benefits. Essential oils, such as lavender and tea tree, in addition to conferring a pleasant aroma, bring therapeutic properties. Apple cider vinegar, with its balancing pH, seals the hair cuticles, promoting shine and softness, while baking soda is effective in removing residue and excess oil.

Choosing the ideal method for your hair type is essential. Normal hair has greater flexibility and can experiment with different options, while dry hair benefits from moisturizing shampoos or methods such as Co-Wash. For oily hair, products with clays and astringent ingredients are ideal, while curly or coily hair adapts better to No Poo or Co-Wash, which preserve natural hydration. Damaged and chemically treated hair requires gentle and moisturizing methods for recovery.

Natural recipes are a practical way to incorporate this care into everyday life. A solid coconut and white clay shampoo, for example, uses a vegetable glycerin base, saponified coconut oil, white clay, and lavender essential oil to offer gentle and nourishing cleansing. For those who prefer the liquid version, the natural aloe vera and chamomile shampoo combines a vegetable base, aloe vera gel, and concentrated chamomile tea, resulting in hydrated and silky hair. The No Poo method with apple cider vinegar is a simple and effective solution: a mixture of apple cider vinegar and water that cleanses and balances the scalp.

To ensure the best results, some tips are valuable. The frequency of washing should respect the characteristics of the hair and lifestyle, usually every two or three days. Water temperature is another important factor: preferring warm or cold water avoids dryness. During washing, gently massaging the scalp stimulates circulation and hair health, while rinsing thoroughly ensures complete removal of products. After cleansing, the use of a natural conditioner helps to moisturize and detangle the hair, complementing the care. Drying also deserves attention: letting the hair dry naturally or using dryers at lower temperatures preserves its structure and vitality.

Natural hair washing goes beyond hygiene; it is care that respects the health of the hair and the environment. By adopting methods and ingredients appropriate to your hair type, you promote hair care that combines beauty, sustainability, and well-being. Each choice is a step towards healthy hair and a more conscious lifestyle.

The transition to natural hair washing can be a significant milestone in a more conscious care routine, bringing benefits that go beyond hair health. In the first few moments, it is common for the hair to need to adapt, as the absence of chemical components alters the dynamics of the scalp. However, over time, the natural balance is restored, revealing stronger, shinier, and healthier hair. This process, however gradual, becomes a valuable learning experience about patience and connection with the needs of one's own body.

By integrating natural washing into daily care, it is noticeable that the effects go beyond aesthetics. The practice encourages a more attentive look at the environmental impact of personal choices, promoting a sustainable lifestyle. Furthermore, each ritual - from the preparation of a handmade shampoo to the careful choice of ingredients - becomes an opportunity for moments of presence and self-care. It is an invitation to slow down and appreciate the simple processes that reverberate positively both in the hair and in overall well-being.

Over time, natural washing ceases to be just an alternative and becomes a lifestyle. Hair responds with vitality, the scalp finds balance, and the environmental impact is minimized. More than a hygiene method, it is a path of reconnection with nature, with health, and with respect for the environment. By adopting this practice, you invest in a beauty that is reflected not only in the hair, but also in more conscious choices aligned with integral care.

# Chapter 24
# Natural Conditioner

Natural conditioner presents itself as a powerful and healthy alternative for hair care, combining the effectiveness of nourishing ingredients with environmental sustainability. Unlike conventional products, which often contain harmful substances such as silicones and parabens, natural conditioner offers a gentler approach that is more aligned with the real needs of the hair. It not only deeply hydrates and nourishes, but also promotes long-term health, allowing hair to better absorb nutrients and remain free of accumulated residue.

The composition of natural conditioners is carefully developed to meet the needs of different hair types, respecting their characteristics and requirements. Ingredients such as vegetable butters, oils rich in fatty acids, and botanical extracts provide intense hydration and repair damage, while lighter elements, such as aloe vera and apple cider vinegar, balance oiliness and strengthen strands. This diversity allows for personalized care, ensuring more efficient and transformative results.

Incorporating the use of natural conditioners into your hair care routine is an essential step towards achieving healthy, shiny, and manageable hair. By opting for these products, you not only promote the regeneration and vitality of your hair, but also contribute to the preservation of the environment. Choosing natural ingredients and avoiding harsh chemicals is an act of conscious self-care that reflects a commitment to genuine beauty and sustainability, enhancing the harmony between health, well-being, and respect for nature.

Natural cosmetics provide a healthy and effective alternative for hair conditioning, using ingredients that hydrate, nourish, and protect hair in a gentle and sustainable way. Unlike conventional products, which often contain harmful chemicals like silicones and parabens, natural conditioners respect hair and environmental health, making them essential allies in a conscious and effective care routine.

Among the main benefits of natural conditioners is their ability to deeply hydrate the hair, restoring its natural moisture and leaving it soft and silky. They nourish the hair with vitamins, minerals and fatty acids, essential for hair health and to stimulate hair growth. In addition, they seal the hair cuticles, reducing frizz, split ends and preventing breakage. The detangling action of these conditioners facilitates brushing, preventing damage, while protection against external agents such as pollution and heat ensures healthy hair in the long term. The result is shiny, manageable, and naturally beautiful hair.

The natural ingredients that make up these conditioners are varied and carefully chosen to meet the needs of different hair types. Vegetable butters, such as shea, cocoa and cupuaçu, provide intense hydration and repair, being ideal for dry and damaged hair. Vegetable oils such as coconut, argan, avocado and jojoba offer nutrition, lightness and shine. Aloe vera, with its moisturizing and soothing properties, is a versatile option to balance oiliness and strengthen strands. Apple cider vinegar, in turn, is known to balance the pH of the scalp and seal the cuticles, giving shine and softness. Essential oils, such as lavender, ylang ylang and rosemary, not only offer a pleasant aroma, but also promote hair health with their therapeutic properties.

Choosing the ideal conditioner depends on the characteristics of the hair. Normal hair can experiment with different combinations of ingredients, while dry hair benefits from nourishing butters and rich oils. Oily hair, on the other hand, requires lighter formulas, such as aloe vera combined with less dense oils, such as jojoba. For curly and coily hair, conditioners rich in butters and oils that help define curls and reduce frizz are ideal. Damaged or chemically treated hair requires repairing ingredients, such as cupuaçu butter and argan oil.

Preparing natural conditioners at home is a practical and economical way to personalize hair care. A conditioner for dry hair, for example, can be made with shea butter, coconut oil, aloe vera and lavender essential oil. The combination of these ingredients deeply hydrates and repairs the hair. For oily hair, a mixture of aloe vera, jojoba oil, apple cider vinegar and rosemary essential oil helps balance oiliness without weighing down the hair. For curly and coily hair, a conditioner with shea butter, coconut oil, castor oil and ylang ylang essential oil provides definition and frizz control.

To maximize the benefits of natural conditioners, some simple practices can be adopted. The application should be done on damp hair, after washing, focusing on the ends, which are more prone to dryness and damage. Leaving the product on for a few minutes allows the nutrients to penetrate the strands, ensuring more effective results. It is important to rinse thoroughly to remove all conditioner and avoid product build-up. Using the conditioner in every wash is essential to keep the hair hydrated and protected. As a finisher, a natural leave-in or finisher can be applied to protect the hair, control frizz and help with styling.

The use of natural conditioners is an investment in hair health and sustainability. By incorporating these practices into your routine, you not only promote the regeneration and vitality of your hair, but also contribute to a positive environmental impact, replacing industrialized products with natural and biodegradable options. The result is complete care that reflects a commitment to conscious beauty and the preservation of nature, enhancing the harmony between aesthetics, health and respect for the environment.

Natural conditioner not only redefines hair care standards, but also redefines the way we relate to our hair and the environment. By replacing industrialized products with natural solutions, we create a deeper connection with the needs of the hair, learning to value it in its authentic form. Each application becomes a moment of self-care and reflection, where simple and natural ingredients offer a rich and transformative experience.

With continued use, hair begins to reveal its true essence, responding healthily and vibrantly to the nutrients offered. This transition, although gradual, teaches that sustainable care is not only effective, but also rewarding. It is as if, by nourishing the strands, we also cultivate patience, awareness and a sense of responsibility for the choices we make, both for our body and for the planet.

Adopting natural conditioners is more than an aesthetic choice; it is a commitment to a balanced and sustainable life. Each strand that reflects shine and health is a reminder that it is possible to take care of yourself without compromising the future. This holistic care not only transforms the hair care routine, but inspires a more conscious and respectful approach to the environment, reinforcing that true beauty lies in choices that promote harmony and well-being.

# Chapter 25
# Natural Hair Masks

Natural hair masks are a powerful and versatile solution for effectively treating hair, using the benefits offered by pure ingredients free of harmful chemical substances. More than just a complement to the care routine, these masks function as intensive treatments that penetrate the hair fiber, promoting deep hydration, nutrition and repair. By avoiding synthetic compounds present in conventional products, they also ensure the preservation of hair health in the long term and minimize environmental impact.

The natural ingredients that make up these masks are rich in vitamins, minerals and antioxidants, essential elements to reverse damage caused by factors such as heat, pollution and chemical treatments. Each component, such as vegetable oils, fruits, butters and herbs, offers specific benefits, catering to different hair types and needs. Regular use of natural hair masks helps rebuild the hair structure, seals the cuticles and improves the texture of the strands, reducing frizz and preventing breakage.

Incorporating natural masks into your hair care routine is not just an aesthetic treatment, but also an act of self-care that promotes well-being. By preparing and applying these treatments, you create a special moment to take care of yourself, strengthening the connection with your own body. In addition, the flexibility of homemade recipes allows you to customize treatments according to your needs, enhancing the results. With this holistic and accessible care, your hair can reach a new level of health, softness and shine, highlighting the beauty that arises from the harmony between nature and science.

Natural hair masks are a valuable resource to promote hair health and beauty, taking advantage of the beneficial properties of natural ingredients that treat hair intensively and without chemical aggression. They offer a holistic and personalized approach, capable of meeting specific needs, such as hydration, nutrition and repair, while protecting the environment and preserving the health of the scalp.

Among the countless benefits of natural hair masks is the ability to deeply hydrate the hair, replenishing lost moisture and restoring shine and softness. Its composition rich in vitamins, minerals and antioxidants nourishes the hair, strengthening the hair fiber and stimulating healthy growth. In addition, ingredients such as vegetable oils and butters help repair damage caused by chemical processes, heat and external factors, while sealing the cuticles, reducing frizz and preventing breakage. Regular use of these masks results in stronger, more manageable and resistant hair, with a healthy and radiant appearance.

The ingredients used in natural masks are varied and versatile, allowing for personalized combinations for different hair types. Fruits such as avocado, banana and papaya are rich sources of vitamins and healthy fats that deeply hydrate and nourish. Honey, natural yogurt and aloe vera have soothing and moisturizing properties, ideal for revitalizing dry and damaged hair. Vegetable oils such as coconut, argan and castor oil are widely recognized for their repairing and strengthening properties, while butters such as shea and cocoa offer intense hydration and protection against external aggressions.

Each hair type can benefit from specific combinations of ingredients. For example, dry hair needs intensive hydration, which can be obtained with masks based on avocado, honey and shea butter. For oily hair, lighter options, such as aloe vera and apple cider vinegar, help balance oiliness and keep hair light and loose. Damaged and chemically treated hair finds recovery in masks with oils such as argan and castor oil, which strengthen and rebuild the hair fiber. Curly and coily hair can use ingredients such as coconut oil and shea butter to define curls and control frizz.

Homemade recipes are practical and effective, allowing the creation of personalized treatments. For dry and parched hair, an avocado and honey mask combines hydration and nutrition: just mix half a mashed avocado with a tablespoon of honey, apply to clean, damp hair, and leave on for 30 minutes before rinsing. For dull and lifeless hair, a mixture of ripe banana with coconut oil restores shine and vitality to the hair. Damaged hair can be treated with a mask of natural yogurt and honey, which strengthens and softens. Those who want to stimulate hair growth can resort to a combination of castor oil and jaborandi extract, applying it to the scalp with a gentle massage to activate circulation.

To enhance the benefits of natural masks, some simple practices are recommended. Applying the mask to clean, damp hair allows nutrients to be absorbed more efficiently. Focus the application on the length and ends, where the hair tends to be more damaged. Using a thermal cap or wrapping the hair in a warm towel during the application time (between 30 minutes and 1 hour) increases the penetration of ingredients into the hair fiber. After treatment, rinsing well with plenty of water is essential to avoid product build-up on the hair.

The frequency of use of the masks varies according to the needs of the hair. For more damaged hair, weekly use or even twice a week is recommended, while normal or less demanding hair can be treated every 15 days. Consistency in use is essential to ensure visible and lasting results.

Natural hair masks are more than an aesthetic treatment; they are a self-care practice that values hair health and promotes well-being. By preparing and applying these masks, you dedicate a moment for yourself, strengthening the connection with your own body and embracing the benefits of nature in its purest form. With conscious and personalized choices, your hair can reach a new level of health and beauty, reflecting the balance between science, nature and care.

Natural hair masks are more than hair treatments; they represent a powerful link between personal care and the benefits that nature offers. Each application is a gesture of kindness to the hair, a way to reverse accumulated damage and restore vitality to the hair structure. The preparation and use of these home treatments not only enhance the results, but also create an experience that transcends conventional self-care, involving it with purpose and meaning.

With continued use, the strands begin to reveal a visible transformation: more shine, strength and malleability become evident, while the hair texture reflects the health that comes from within. More than an aesthetic resource, natural masks teach the importance of patience and consistency, as it is in the time dedicated to care that the most profound results manifest themselves. By exploring simple and accessible ingredients, you approach a routine that balances efficiency and respect for the environment.

Adopting natural hair masks as part of your routine is not just a choice for tangible results, but also a way to cultivate complete well-being. Hair care reflects a holistic approach, in which health, aesthetics and connection with nature are intertwined. Thus, each home treatment becomes a celebration of authentic beauty, revealing that true care lies in conscious choices and the affection dedicated to oneself.

# Chapter 26
## Natural Hair Finishing

Natural hair finishing represents an essential milestone in the hair care journey, elevating the health and appearance of strands to new heights. This process utilizes natural ingredients and methods that respect both the integrity of the hair and the environment, eliminating dependence on harsh chemicals. With a focus on promoting hydration, protection, and definition, natural finishing not only beautifies the strands but also deeply nourishes and strengthens them, making it a sustainable and effective choice.

By replacing synthetic substances, such as silicones and parabens, with natural alternatives, it is possible to preserve the hair structure and ensure efficient absorption of nutrients, guaranteeing complete and healthy care.

The benefits of natural finishing go beyond aesthetics; they encompass a holistic approach that combines beauty and well-being. Ingredients such as vegetable oils, butters, and natural extracts form a protective barrier against external aggressions, such as pollution and heat, while sealing moisture within the strands. In addition, their shaping action allows you to enhance curls, waves, or straight hairstyles in a gentle and natural way, without weighing them down or causing buildup. Each hair type finds specific solutions within this practice, whether for frizz control in straight hair or curl definition in curly hair. This versatility makes natural finishing a democratic and accessible choice, regardless of individual hair characteristics.

Another fundamental aspect of this approach lies in its ability to be personalized, allowing each person to adapt natural finishers to the specific needs of their hair. From simple recipes, such as gels and creams made with everyday ingredients, to more elaborate blends with rare oils and aromatic herbs, natural finishing offers almost endless possibilities. This flexibility encourages a closer and more conscious relationship with personal care, promoting a connection between health, aesthetics, and sustainability. Adopting this practice is not only a step towards natural beauty but also a commitment to a lifestyle that values holistic care and harmony with the environment.

Natural finishing offers several advantages that transcend aesthetics, constituting true holistic hair care. This approach synergistically combines protection, hydration, and definition, using ingredients that do not harm the strands and promote long-term health and beauty. For example, natural finishers create a protective layer against external aggressions, such as sunlight, pollution, and heat, while sealing in moisture and deeply nourishing the hair. Ingredients such as vegetable oils, natural butters, and botanical extracts play an essential role in this process, providing a healthy shine and a soft, smooth texture.

In addition to protecting, these products act on the shaping of the strands, ensuring that curls, waves, or even straight hairstyles gain a unique definition without the stiffness of synthetic stylers. A good example is flaxseed gel, which defines curls in a light and natural way, and coconut cream, known for its ability to nourish and moisturize while shaping. These finishers also have properties that control frizz, a result of the combination of efficient hydration and sealing of the cuticles, reducing the frizzy appearance and leaving the strands more aligned.

For a personalized approach, it is important to consider the specific characteristics of each hair type. For example, those with straight hair should opt for light finishers, such as jojoba oil or herbal sprays, which do not weigh down the strands. For wavy hair, finishers that define waves and control frizz, such as flaxseed gel or coconut cream, are more suitable. Curly and coily hair, in turn, requires products that offer greater hydration and control, such as shea butter and coconut oil. For damaged or chemically treated hair, it is essential to invest in restorative finishers, such as aloe vera or cupuaçu butter, which help in the recovery of the strands.

One of the great advantages of natural finishing is the possibility of creating your own products at home, using accessible and natural ingredients. For example, flaxseed gel is easy to prepare: just boil 1/4 cup of flaxseed in 1 cup of filtered water for about 5 minutes, stirring occasionally. After straining the gel through a thin cloth, it can be stored in a glass jar in the refrigerator. To apply, spread the gel on clean, damp hair, shaping the curls with your fingers.

Another practical and nutritious option is the coconut combing cream, which combines 1/2 cup of coconut milk with 1 tablespoon of coconut oil and 1 tablespoon of cornstarch. The preparation consists of mixing the coconut milk with the starch in a pan and bringing it to a low heat, stirring until thickened. After removing from heat, add the coconut oil and mix well. Store in a clean, dry container, and apply to clean, damp strands, shaping them as desired.

For those looking for a refreshing and fragrant touch, the herbal spray is ideal. Use 100 ml of filtered water, 1 tablespoon of fresh rosemary and 1 tablespoon of fresh lavender. Start by boiling the water and adding the herbs. After turning off the heat, cover the mixture and let it steep for 30 minutes. Strain the liquid and store it in a spray bottle. This spray can be applied to both damp and dry hair, helping to finish the hairstyle with lightness and freshness.

For natural finishing to be even more effective, some tips are essential. It is crucial to apply the right amount of finisher, adapted to the hair type and length of the strands. Start with a small amount, distributing evenly from the length to the ends. During application, use your fingers, a wide-tooth comb, or a brush to gently shape the strands. Drying also makes a difference: letting your hair air dry helps preserve moisture, but those who prefer to dry it faster can use a diffuser to highlight curls and waves.

Finally, after drying, a light vegetable oil, such as argan oil or jojoba oil, can be applied to give extra shine and control any remaining frizz. This last step closes the care cycle, ensuring that the strands are not only beautiful but also healthy and protected.

By adopting natural finishing, each person begins to exercise greater control over what they apply to their hair, strengthening the relationship between beauty and sustainability. This practice is not just an aesthetic choice, but a commitment to well-being and connection with the environment. The result is complete care that combines functionality, personalization, and a deep respect for hair health and nature.

Natural finishing redefines the way we connect to our hair and the environment around us. This practice goes beyond styling or controlling the strands; it is intentional care that respects the unique characteristics of each hair type and promotes its long-term health. By opting for natural methods and ingredients, you not only reduce exposure to harmful chemicals, but also contribute to more sustainable and environmentally friendly practices.

Over time, the results speak for themselves: hair that shines with vitality, softness that can be felt to the touch, and a texture that reflects care from the inside out. Personalization is one of the most rewarding aspects of this approach, allowing each person to adapt recipes and techniques according to their needs and preferences. This process also strengthens the connection with self-care, transforming the simple act of finishing the strands into a meaningful ritual.

Adopting natural finishing is more than a product choice; it is a philosophy of care that balances health, aesthetics, and respect for nature. Each strand shaped with natural ingredients reflects a commitment to conscious choices and a celebration of authentic beauty. In this process, what emerges is not only healthy hair, but also a more harmonious and sustainable attitude towards the world.

# Chapter 27
# Hair Loss

Hair loss, although common, raises concerns that go beyond aesthetics, often indicating deeper changes in the body. This process can be influenced by internal and external factors that, when not identified and treated, significantly compromise hair health. It is essential to understand that the natural loss of strands is part of the hair renewal cycle, but when the amount of hair lost exceeds the usual limits, it is a warning sign. From this perspective, taking care of the scalp and adopting strategies that promote body balance become indispensable actions to preserve the strength and vitality of the hair.

Among the most frequent causes of hair loss are genetic conditions, hormonal changes, nutritional deficiencies, and the impact of stress on a daily basis. In addition, exposure to aggressive chemical processes and improper use of cosmetic products can weaken the hair structure, aggravating the loss. To combat these factors, natural cosmetics emerge as a powerful ally, integrating treatments that strengthen the strands with self-care practices that promote general well-being. This holistic approach favors not only the interruption of the problem, but also a healthier environment for the growth of new strands.

Adopting natural practices in combating hair loss brings benefits that go beyond reducing hair loss. Ingredients such as vegetable oils, stimulating herbs, and botanical extracts not only strengthen the strands but also help restore scalp balance. Products such as rosemary tonics and aloe vera masks offer regenerating and moisturizing properties that revitalize hair follicles, while regular massages stimulate circulation and increase the absorption of essential nutrients. These strategies, combined with a balanced diet and the reduction of stressors, form the basis for hair recovery. By treating hair health in an integrated way, it is possible not only to contain the loss, but also to cultivate stronger and healthier strands.

Hair loss is a topic that goes beyond aesthetic concern, involving multiple factors that can affect hair health. Several elements contribute to the weakening and loss of strands, and understanding their causes is the first step towards effective treatment. Among the main factors are genetic predispositions, hormonal changes, nutritional deficiencies, and the impact of daily stress. In addition, the use of harsh chemicals and hairstyles that strain the strands also play a significant role in this process.

Genetic predisposition is one of the best-known causes of hair loss, with androgenetic alopecia, which affects both men and women, being noteworthy. This type of loss is progressive and hereditary, often manifesting on the top of the head and temples.

Hormonal factors can trigger significant changes in the hair cycle, being common during pregnancy, postpartum, menopause, or in cases of thyroid dysfunction. Changes in hormone levels weaken the strands and often result in diffuse loss.

Another critical aspect is nutrition. Deficiencies in iron, zinc, biotin, vitamin D, and protein directly affect hair health, making strands more susceptible to breakage and loss. To top it off, physical and emotional stress acts as a powerful trigger, releasing hormones that interrupt the hair growth cycle, contributing to a phenomenon known as telogen effluvium, characterized by temporary and accentuated loss.

In addition to internal causes, daily habits also have an influence. Frequent use of chemical processes, such as straightening, dyeing, and perming, damages the hair structure. Similarly, very tight hairstyles, such as braids or ponytails tightly tied, create tension on the strands, leading to traction alopecia.

To deal with these problems, natural cosmetics offer effective and integrative solutions. Products based on vegetable oils, herbs, and botanical extracts strengthen the strands and restore scalp balance. For example, rosemary, known for its stimulating properties, improves blood circulation in the scalp, encouraging hair growth. Aloe vera, in turn, is highly moisturizing and regenerating, aiding in the recovery of damaged strands.

To put these solutions into practice, some natural recipes can be incorporated into the routine. A rosemary hair tonic is easy to prepare and highly effective. Boil a cup of filtered water, add fresh rosemary leaves and let it steep for 30 minutes. After straining, mix with a cup of apple cider vinegar and store in a dark bottle. This tonic should be applied to the clean scalp, with a gentle massage, twice a day.

Another option is the onion and aloe vera hair mask, ideal for revitalizing hair follicles. Mix a small grated onion with two tablespoons of aloe vera gel. Apply to the scalp, massaging gently, and leave on for 30 minutes before rinsing with a natural shampoo.

For those looking for a deeper treatment, castor oil and jaborandi hair oil is an excellent choice. Mix two tablespoons of castor oil with one tablespoon of jaborandi extract. Apply to the scalp and massage gently. After 30 minutes, wash your hair to remove excess oil. This treatment nourishes the strands and stimulates healthy growth.

In addition to these practices, it is essential to adopt habits that preserve hair health. A balanced diet, rich in essential nutrients such as iron, biotin, and protein, is indispensable. Controlling stress also plays an important role; techniques such as meditation, yoga, or physical exercise help balance the body and mind, reducing the negative impacts on the hair cycle.

To avoid further damage, it is advisable to minimize the use of harsh chemicals and avoid excessive heat tools, such as hair dryers and flat irons. Choosing natural shampoos and conditioners, free of sulfates and parabens, contributes to gentler and more effective care for the scalp and strands. In addition, wearing looser hairstyles helps prevent traction alopecia.

Finally, consulting a dermatologist is essential for cases of persistent or excessive hair loss. A professional can identify underlying causes and propose specific treatments, such as supplementation or more advanced therapies. This follow-up is essential to ensure that the problem is treated at the root, promoting lasting and sustainable hair recovery.

Caring for your hair is a process that requires dedication and attention to detail, but the results are rewarding. By combining natural practices, a healthy routine, and professional monitoring, it is possible to transform the relationship with the strands, restoring the strength, vitality, and beauty of the hair.

Hair loss can be seen as a sign that the body demands full attention, combining specific care for the strands with a broader approach to health and balance. Understanding the causes and adopting natural strategies, such as tonics and masks based on regenerating ingredients, is an important step in reversing the problem and strengthening the hair. These treatments not only treat the symptoms, but help build a solid foundation for healthy, long-lasting growth, always respecting the individuality of each person.

Throughout the process, incorporating healthy habits becomes essential to sustain the results obtained. A diet rich in essential nutrients, combined with practices that reduce stress, such as meditation or physical activities, reinforces the impact of natural treatments. Small changes, such as replacing conventional products with cosmetics free of harsh substances, also create a more favorable environment for hair health, reducing external aggressions that contribute to hair loss.

More than an aesthetic concern, dealing with hair loss is a path of self-knowledge and integral care. Each strengthened strand is a reflection of the balance achieved, and each practice adopted symbolizes a commitment to one's own well-being. Thus, the treatment of hair loss is transformed into a journey that connects the health of the strands to the harmony of body and mind, revealing a beauty that goes beyond the surface.

# Chapter 28
# Dandruff and Scalp

Scalp health plays an essential role in maintaining beautiful and vibrant hair. Problems such as dandruff, itching, and sensitivity often indicate imbalances that go beyond the surface, directly affecting the quality of the strands. Dandruff, for example, is characterized by excessive flaking of the scalp and can be the result of factors such as uncontrolled fungal growth, excess oil, dryness, or even reactions to harsh chemicals. By addressing these problems holistically, it is possible not only to alleviate symptoms but also to restore the vitality and balance of the scalp in a lasting way.

One of the pillars for treating and preventing dandruff is the adoption of practices that promote a healthy environment for the hair from the root. Natural ingredients such as essential oils, botanical extracts, and clays stand out for their antifungal, anti-inflammatory, and moisturizing properties, being able to balance the scalp microbiome while strengthening the strands. In addition, simple techniques, such as regular massages, exfoliation, and hydration with appropriate products, help to remove impurities, stimulate circulation, and deeply nourish the scalp. This integrated care improves not only the appearance of the hair but also its overall health, effectively reducing the incidence of problems such as dandruff.

When treating the scalp, it is also important to consider internal factors that can contribute to the appearance of dandruff and other imbalances. A balanced diet, rich in nutrients such as zinc, omega-3, and B vitamins, can have a significant impact on the health of the hair and scalp. Similarly, reducing stress and maintaining an active lifestyle help regulate hormone levels and strengthen the immune system, minimizing the conditions that favor the appearance of hair problems. Scalp care, therefore, should be understood as a combination of external treatments and lifestyle adjustments, providing more complete and sustainable results.

Dandruff, characterized by excessive flaking of the scalp, is a common hair problem that can cause discomfort and impact self-esteem. Although often treated as a simple aesthetic problem, its origin is often linked to deeper imbalances, such as the excessive presence of the fungus Malassezia globosa, changes in oil production, or even inflammatory conditions such as seborrheic dermatitis. Factors such as dry scalp, sensitivities to chemicals, and diseases such as psoriasis, which require a careful and personalized approach, can also contribute.

Among the causes of dandruff, the fungus Malassezia globosa is one of the main agents, naturally present on the scalp, but capable of excessive proliferation when it finds favorable conditions, such as excess sebum or changes in pH. This proliferation can lead to irritation, inflammation, and flaking. On the other hand, extreme dryness can also cause flaking, although it is usually associated with itching and sensitivity.

External factors, such as the use of harsh chemicals, represent another challenge. Substances such as sulfates, parabens, and silicones, commonly present in conventional cosmetics, can trigger adverse reactions, irritating the scalp and aggravating dandruff. Similarly, chronic stress can play an important role, destabilizing hormonal and immune balance, which favors the appearance of hair problems.

To treat and prevent dandruff, natural cosmetics offer a holistic approach, using ingredients that balance the scalp and promote healthy hair. Products with antifungal properties, such as tea tree essential oil, act directly to control the Malassezia globosa fungus, while moisturizing elements, such as aloe vera and coconut oil, help restore the scalp's natural barrier. Apple cider vinegar, in turn, is a powerful ally to balance pH and control oiliness.

The care routine begins with the choice of gentle products free of harsh agents. A natural anti-dandruff shampoo can be easily prepared at home by combining effective ingredients. Mix half a cup of vegetable shampoo base with a tablespoon of green clay and ten drops of tea tree essential oil. This shampoo should be applied to wet hair, massaged gently, and left on for a few minutes before rinsing. Green clay purifies and controls oiliness, while tea tree effectively combats dandruff.

Another simple and effective treatment is apple cider vinegar hair tonic. Mix half a cup of apple cider vinegar with half a cup of filtered water and apply to clean scalp. Massage gently and leave on for 15 minutes before washing your hair with a natural shampoo. This tonic helps balance the scalp microbiome, reducing flaking and promoting healthy shine to hair.

For deep hydration, the aloe vera and coconut oil mask is ideal. Combine half a cup of aloe vera gel with a quarter cup of coconut oil and apply to hair and scalp, massaging gently. Leave on for 30 minutes and rinse with natural shampoo. This mask is especially effective for dry and sensitive scalps as it deeply moisturizes and reduces itching.

In addition to topical treatments, it is essential to adopt a care routine that includes regular washing with shampoos appropriate for your hair type, weekly exfoliation with gentle scrubs to remove dead cells, and regular scalp massages to stimulate blood circulation. These practices not only help fight dandruff but also promote a healthy environment for hair growth.

Lifestyle also plays a crucial role in controlling dandruff. A balanced diet, rich in whole foods, fresh vegetables, fruits, nuts, and seeds, provides essential nutrients such as zinc, omega-3s, and B vitamins, which are essential for scalp health. Reducing the consumption of processed foods and foods rich in sugar also contributes to the balance of the hair microbiome.

Controlling stress is equally important. Techniques such as meditation, yoga, or regular physical activity help regulate hormone levels and strengthen the immune system, minimizing the conditions that favor dandruff. It is important to remember that in more severe or persistent cases, consulting a dermatologist is essential to identify the underlying cause and receive specialized guidance.

Taking care of the scalp is an investment in the health and beauty of your hair. By adopting natural practices, maintaining a consistent care routine, and adjusting your lifestyle, it is possible not only to combat dandruff but also to improve the quality of the strands in a lasting way. This holistic approach promotes not only immediate relief of symptoms but also a sustainable balance, ensuring healthier, more beautiful, and problem-free hair.

The balance between external and internal care is essential to keep the scalp healthy and dandruff-free. Natural products, combined with appropriate daily practices, are powerful allies to restore hair health. However, the key to consistent results is patience and perseverance, as the scalp takes time to respond to positive changes. Therefore, adopting a personalized approach that takes into account the specific needs of each person is crucial to achieve the desired balance.

Furthermore, understanding that scalp health reflects the overall well-being of the body can transform the way we view hair care. A well-nourished and harmonious organism has a greater capacity to fight inflammation and imbalances, creating ideal conditions for hair regeneration and the prevention of problems such as dandruff. Thus, scalp care should not be seen only as a beauty routine, but as an integral part of a healthy lifestyle.

By incorporating these practices, the journey to a healthy scalp becomes a transformative experience, both physically and emotionally. Each gesture of care not only promotes stronger and more beautiful hair but also reflects a commitment to oneself. The combination of dedication, knowledge, and conscious choices creates a safe path to a harmonious relationship between health, well-being, and self-esteem.

# Chapter 29
# White Hair

White hair, more than a natural milestone of aging, is a unique expression of individuality and the passage of time. They appear when melanocytes, responsible for the production of melanin, reduce or cease their activity, which results in the gradual loss of pigmentation. Although often associated with maturity, they can appear prematurely due to genetic factors, nutritional imbalances, stress, or health conditions. Regardless of the cause, white hair requires specific care, not only to preserve its appearance but also to ensure the health and vitality of the strands.

Over the years, white hair tends to become drier, more porous, and vulnerable to environmental damage. Therefore, it is essential to adopt routines that favor hydration, nutrition, and protection of the strands. Natural masks rich in vegetable oils, such as coconut and argan, and moisturizing ingredients, such as aloe vera, can restore softness and shine, while specific products to neutralize yellowing preserve the vibrant and luminous tone of white hair. In addition, protecting hair from the sun and minimizing the use of excessive heat contribute to maintaining its integrity and preventing damage.

For those who wish to camouflage white hair, natural alternatives, such as henna and coloring herbs, offer a healthy and sustainable solution. Unlike chemical dyes, these options do not harm the hair or scalp, promoting gradual coloring rich in nuances. On the other hand, assuming white hair with confidence and elegance has become an increasingly celebrated choice, valuing authenticity and natural beauty. With proper care, it is possible to transform white hair into a symbol of style, strength, and individuality, reflecting a beauty that transcends standards and embraces the uniqueness of each person.

The daily practice of facial cleansing is essential to ensure the health and vitality of the skin. More than just an aesthetic habit, it is a preventive and restorative measure that protects against clogged pores and adverse conditions such as acne, irritation, and signs of premature aging. In addition, the choice of natural methods provides special care, where the skin is treated with respect, free of chemical aggressions, and in harmony with sustainable principles.

Facial cleansing is not limited to removing visible residues. It is an act of deep care, which acts on different levels of the skin. By performing it twice a day, morning and night, its benefits accumulate and transform skin health. Impurities such as dirt, pollution particles, and makeup are effectively removed, preventing clogged pores and reducing the formation of blackheads and pimples. Removing excess oil is also crucial, especially in the T-zone – which includes the forehead, nose, and chin – areas prone to excessive shine and acne.

This ritual goes beyond simple cleansing: it promotes cell renewal by eliminating dead cells, restoring a youthful, radiant appearance and even texture to the skin. The effectiveness of other treatment products, such as moisturizers, serums, and masks, is amplified on properly cleansed skin, as nutrients and actives find a clear path to act deeply. In addition, cleansing plays an essential role in balancing the skin's pH and supporting healthy bacterial flora, which are fundamental aspects of maintaining long-term skin health.

In natural cosmetics, the approach to facial cleansing is done gently and effectively, respecting the integrity of the skin. Methods such as cleansing milks stand out for their moisturizing and soothing properties, being ideal for dry and sensitive skin. They combine vegetable oils such as sweet almond oil, butters such as shea butter, and rose or chamomile hydrosols, offering a rich and comforting experience. Natural soaps, made with vegetable oils and clays, meet the needs of oily skin well, balancing oiliness without causing dryness. For combination or oily skin, cleansing gels based on aloe vera, green tea, and tea tree hydrosols provide freshness and lightness. Finally, micellar waters, composed of micelles that capture impurities, adapt to all skin types, being practical and effective.

Choosing the ideal facial cleansing product depends on analyzing your skin type and its specific needs. Dry and sensitive skin benefits from moisturizing and soothing formulas, while oily and combination skin requires compositions with astringent ingredients.

Normal skin, in turn, offers greater freedom of choice, just observe how it responds to different products.

The facial cleansing method involves simple but fundamental steps to ensure clean and healthy skin. The first step is to remove any makeup present. A natural makeup remover, such as coconut oil or micellar water, can be used to dissolve makeup, preparing the skin for a deeper cleanse. With your face moistened in warm or cold water, apply the chosen cleansing product, spreading it gently in circular motions for about a minute. This massage not only cleanses but stimulates blood circulation, contributing to skin revitalization. Rinsing with clean water removes the product and any remaining residue, leaving the skin ready for the final step: drying. Here, it is essential to use a soft towel and avoid rubbing, so as not to damage the skin.

Natural methods offer not only effectiveness but also the possibility of creating personalized products at home, with simple and accessible ingredients. For example, for dry skin, a cleansing milk can be prepared by mixing two tablespoons of sweet almond oil, one tablespoon of shea butter, two tablespoons of rose hydrosol, and ten drops of lavender essential oil. The result is a nourishing and softening product, which can be applied with the hands or with a cotton pad, gently removing impurities.

For oily skin, natural soap is an excellent choice. Starting with a vegetable glycerin base, add a tablespoon of green clay, one of coconut oil, and ten drops of tea tree essential oil. This soap not only cleanses but also helps balance oiliness, promoting more even skin. The preparation process is simple: the glycerin base is melted in a water bath, the ingredients are incorporated, and the mixture is poured into molds, where it dries for 24 hours before being used.

An ideal cleansing gel for combination skin can be made by combining half a cup of aloe vera gel, a tablespoon of witch hazel extract, and ten drops of lemon essential oil. The result is a light and refreshing product that revitalizes the skin while removing excess oil. Application is simple: just massage the gel on your face and rinse.

These methods show how it is possible to incorporate skin care practices that, in addition to being efficient, value natural ingredients and promote well-being. Facial cleansing thus becomes more than an obligation: a moment of self-care that renews not only the skin but also the connection with one's own body.

White hair, whether adopted naturally or transformed through natural colors, carries with it a unique narrative that reflects history, style, and self-confidence. Caring for these strands goes beyond aesthetics, involving special attention to texture, shine, and resistance. Choosing appropriate products, combined with simple and effective routines, can revitalize the strands, highlighting their unique beauty and transforming them into an expression of authenticity.

The transition to assuming white hair, when done intentionally, also becomes an act of freedom and acceptance. This process is an invitation to deconstruct conventional beauty standards and embrace one's own aesthetic, marked by the courage to celebrate naturalness. With the right care, it is possible to enhance the charm of white hair, exploring its nuances and creating a look that translates individuality and strength.

Finally, regardless of individual choices, white hair symbolizes more than just a physical change. They represent a journey of transformation and maturity, where each strand is a testament to lived experiences. Treating this hair with care and attention reflects not only a concern with appearance but also a deep respect for one's own history and the beauty it carries.

# Epilogue

Reaching the end of this reading is not just closing a book, but the beginning of a new perception of beauty, health, and self-care. You have traveled a path that reveals not only formulas and practices but a lifestyle based on balance, respect, and authenticity.

In each chapter, you were introduced to a world where the simple becomes powerful and the natural is revealed as the answer to many of the challenges we face in our search for well-being. The beauty that this book defends is not ephemeral or superficial, but rooted in choices that nourish and sustain body and soul.

More than cosmetic recipes or explanations about ingredients, this content offers a philosophy of life. Each essential oil, each clay, and each ritual described here carries a message: that caring for the body is a reflection of caring for the world. By valuing natural ingredients and sustainable practices, you not only transform your skin but also contribute to a more balanced and healthy planet.

This book has shown that true beauty is a harmonious dance between the inner and outer self. It is not the temporary glow of a chemical, but the authentic glow that comes from an aligned life, where health, self-care, and consciousness walk together.

Now is the time to take this learning beyond the pages. Every little gesture - choosing a healthier food, creating a skincare ritual, or simply taking a deep breath in nature - reinforces the idea that beauty is in everyday actions.

If there is one essential lesson this book leaves, it is that self-care is an act of love that reverberates in all areas of life. That by nourishing your skin, you feed your soul. That by valuing the natural, you celebrate the simplicity and strength that come from the earth.

The journey through holistic beauty does not end here. In fact, it is just beginning. May each day be an opportunity to deepen this connection with yourself and the world around you. And may you remember that self-care is not a luxury, but a necessity, a gift you give yourself and everyone who has the privilege of sharing life by your side.

With wishes for a life illuminated by your authentic beauty.

www.ingramcontent.com/pod-product-compliance
Lightning Source LLC
LaVergne TN
LVHW040056080526
838202LV00045B/3666